Leadership Dubai Style

Habits to lead by!

[signature]

ALSO BY DR. TOMMY WEIR

10 tips for Leading in the Middle East
The Cheeseburger Theory and other leadership observations

Leadership Dubai Style
The habits to achieve remarkable success

Dr. Tommy Weir

EMLC PRESS

Copyright © 2015 by Dr. Tommy Weir

P R E S S
Indianapolis, Indiana
United States of America

ISBN: **978 0 996 63750 3**
Library of Congress Control Number: **2015912026**

Leadership Dubai Style *is dedicated to our leader, His Highness Sheikh Mohammed bin Rashid Al Maktoum, vice president and prime minister of the United Arab Emirates and ruler of Dubai, the leaders before him—his father, Sheikh Rashid, grandfather Sheikh Saeed, great-grandfather Sheikh Maktoum, as well as Sheikh Hasher bin Maktoum and Sheikh Maktoum bin Butti, and the leaders who will come.*

And, to His Highness Sheikh Ahmed bin Saeed Al Maktoum for his support of Leadership Dubai Style *—thank you!*

Challenge

By Sheikh Mohammed bin Rashid Al Maktoum

In the race for excellence, I have competed with the finest;
only those with the greatest of souls yearn for first.
He who desires to gain must constantly strive
for today's achievements must surpass past wonders.
A lion in majestic repose is not necessarily a great hunter.
It's the blood on his teeth that speaks of his deeds.
You who tell of glorious feats,
record our youth raising their flags and banners with pride.
Horsemen and trainers, do not worry,
for we will not ever accept anything but first place.
I love challenge, I sing with joy to meet it.
Familiar hardship fires me.
I exhausted the wearied earth, yet never did I tire.
I drained the birds of the sky and wore down my critics.
I lead and persevere; others lead and flag.
The victor must eclipse the strongest in the field.
At the critical time, even a seasoned campaigner
can be struck by fear when called to face the challenge.
Anxious, he will not eat or drink.
Tormented, he may forfeit the comfort of sleep.
Yet we rode together, cantering horses.
The earth was our saddle, reins and bridle.
Every horse knows the rider on its back
only the most decisive can steer the reins through hardship.
We won and through us all Arabs gain.
We offer our victory as a gift to our people.[1]

A Note about Honorific Title Citations in
Leadership Dubai Style

While it is customary to refer to a Ruler using his full title—for example, His Highness Sheikh Mohammed bin Rashid Al Maktoum, vice president and prime minister of the United Arab Emirates and ruler of Dubai—I have decided to use the reference "Sheikh Mohammed" for ease of reading. When there are more than two Rulers with the same first name, I refer to the Ruler in question by his first and father's name—for example, Sheikh Maktoum bin Butti, Sheikh Maktoum bin Hasher, and Sheikh Maktoum bin Rashid. This decision was taken to preserve the honor due to the Ruler and to make the reading as pleasant as possible for you.

Also please note that, per tradition, "Ruler" and "Sheikh" are capitalized throughout the book as a sign of respect.

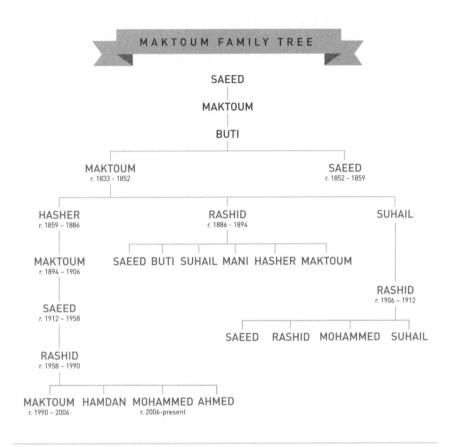

MAKTOUM FAMILY TREE

SAEED

MAKTOUM

BUTI

MAKTOUM
r. 1833 - 1852

SAEED
r. 1852 - 1859

HASHER
r. 1859 – 1886

RASHID
r. 1886 - 1894

SUHAIL

MAKTOUM
r. 1894 – 1906

SAEED   BUTI   SUHAIL   MANI   HASHER   MAKTOUM

RASHID
r. 1906 – 1912

SAEED
r. 1912 – 1958

SAEED   RASHID   MOHAMMED   SUHAIL

RASHID
r. 1958 – 1990

MAKTOUM   HAMDAN   MOHAMMED   AHMED
r. 1990 – 2006   r. 2006-present

VII

TABLE OF CONTENTS

ACKNOWLEDGMENTS

Basma, thank you! Your endless patience while I write reaffirms that you are my biggest cheerleader and supporter. If it weren't for you taking over when I mentally disappear into the words in my head, *Leadership Dubai Style* would not be a reality.

Tricia, my editor, as bizarre as it may sound, thank you for the torture you put me through to turn my scratches on the page into this book. *Leadership Dubai Style* is better because of you!

Mounir, and the Lowe MENA team, thank you for making *Leadership Dubai Style* beautiful. Because of you the cover is a masterpiece!

Farid, thank you for your support on *Leadership Dubai Style* at the beginning of what proved to be a longer than anticipated and much richer than ever dreamed of journey.

I only wish I had the space to say thank you individually to every person I interviewed while researching this book. Truly, *Leadership Dubai Style* wouldn't exist without you. Your insights and experiences provided the basis for this model. Since there isn't room to say it individually, I'll say collectively on behalf of the readers, THANK YOU!

And, what an honor it is to climb on the shoulders of historians who dug through the archives and made the history of Dubai accessible. And a special thanks to fellow author Graeme Wilson, who provided a broad-stroke view of Dubai's history.

INTRODUCTION

Every now and then a story comes along that absolutely rivets you. Dubai is one of those for me. This eye-popping city caught my attention well before ever stepping foot here in 2003 and even more so after making it my home a couple of years later. Five decades ago, this now-global city was nothing more than an obscure, isolated speck on the Arabian Sea. Today you can Jet Ski around a man-made island, eat lunch half a mile in the sky, and enjoy happy hour at the horse races.

When it comes to Dubai's dizzying, gravity-defying growth, Farid Mohammad Ahmad Al Bastaki, former secretary general to the Board of Directors of Dubai World, says it best: "In my opinion, the growth has been much faster than anybody could ever imagine. We are right to say that we surprised ourselves."[2] Al Bastaki should know: a native Dubaian, his life transcends the city's amazing metamorphosis from simple fishing village to glamorous magnet for tourism and trade.

According to the MasterCard 2014 Global Destination Cities Index,[3] Dubai is the fifth most visited city in the world (international visitors), ahead of even New York. In the same year, it retained the honor of being the world's second most important international shopping destination.[4] Also in 2014, Dubai International Airport overtook London's Heathrow in becoming the world's top hub for international travel. Of course this is in addition to having the world's ninth-busiest seaport, the world's tallest tower, and the world's most visited lifestyle destination—Dubai Mall, attracting more visitors than Disney World's Magic Kingdom and the Eiffel Tower.

Yet two generations ago, homes in Dubai didn't have running water or electricity. There was no airport, there were no hotels, and the only infrastructure was a silt-clogged creek in desperate need of repair. Today Dubai is a sought-after destination—a connecting point—with more than two million residents (88 percent of whom are expatriates). Between 1975 and 1995 the population quadrupled, and since 1995 it has doubled. Over thirteen million tourists travel to see Dubai for themselves each year.[5]

So the question is: How did Dubai go from a devastated pearling village to high-flying global powerhouse in less than fifty years?

As someone classically trained in observing human behavior, and having spent the past twenty-five years studying leaders for a living, I tend to eavesdrop on conversations with ease. Oftentimes I'll be sitting in local cafés, "accidentally" listening to how people credit oil wealth with fostering Dubai's success. But this is a factually flawed conclusion. Dubai is the poorest among the Gulf Cooperation Council (GCC) petrochemical producers. The UAE's (United Arab Emirates') neighbors—Saudi Arabia, Qatar, and Kuwait—all pump a disproportionate share of the world's oil and gas, especially when compared with their populations.[6] As a result, all these countries enjoy massive sovereign wealth funds. Yet, Dubai has very limited oil reserves.

So, how did Dubai do it? How did Dubai become, well,

I can't think of any other word to describe it than . . . Dubai?

Leadership! The secret to Dubai's success is solely based on leadership. Other than leadership, how else do you explain Dubai's incredible evolution?

But this isn't your typical government leadership, nor for that matter corporate leadership (although the Ruler is casually referred to as the "CEO of Dubai").[7] It's not the type of leadership that's taught in the sacred classrooms of the world's top business schools—many of which now have satellite campuses in Dubai—or that you'll find in a popular management book. No, this contrarian, highly effective form of leadership is quite simply, leadership Dubai style.

Over this past decade, living and working in Dubai, I watched with awe as the skyline mushroomed right out of the sand, building after building. As a leadership scholar and advisor to CEOs, I yearned to know the leadership formula behind Dubai's success. So did my clients. Over and over they asked me, "How did Dubai do it?" How *did* Dubai do it? I had to know! And so did the CEOs I work with, who wanted to copy whatever Dubai was doing.

So, I set out on a quest—to discover the secrets behind Dubai's leadership model. Just as I started to crack the code in 2008, the Global Financial Crisis hit. Like everyone, I held my breath, wondering if my infatuation was ill founded. Reluctantly, I hit the pause button on my research and waited to see how Dubai would react.

What happened next confirmed there is indeed something unique and amazing here, something worth investigating. Dubai recovered! Actually it did more than recover: Dubai emerged from the Global Financial Crisis stronger and more focused than ever before. Highways that emptied in 2009 filled back up. The once in-demand restaurants, where during the crisis you could get a table any night of the week, quickly returned to needing reservations weeks in advance. Tourism grew, trade soared, and companies started hiring again. Property values that halved, recovered. Dubai grew and continues to expand, with healthy comparative GDP growth each year since 2010. This remarkable turnaround drove me to spend the next three years researching and analyzing Dubai's leadership secrets. I kept digging and digging, eventually unearthing a replicable leadership model that I could share with you, businesses, and governments.

Warning: this model *is* going to change the way you look at leadership. It puts what's traditionally taught about leadership to the test. But the proof is in the pudding. This model *should* be different, drastically different, because Dubai's achievements outpace all the indices. To achieve different results, like Dubai has, you need to do something different—you have to lead differently.

After the 2008 Global Financial Crisis, I dug deeper into the city's history and discovered that Dubai's leadership secrets aren't just from the last decade; they've been present since day one, when the Maktoums migrated to Dubai in 1833. This discovery altered the course of my research, forcing me to take a more holistic look at the history of leadership in Dubai. My focus extended, my findings became comprehensive rather than generational. In the end, *Leadership Dubai Style* shares Dubai's leadership habits so others, like you, may apply them as well and hopefully experience equally mesmerizing results.

If you've ever wanted to know just how Dubai happened, you're about to find out. In the following pages, you'll see exactly how Dubai was built, with behind-the-scenes access to some of the city's most prominent movers and shakers. This inspiring model will hopefully trigger you to form the same habits as these exemplary leaders. While this book focuses on Dubai, it is much more than being about the city or creating an equally spectacular metropolis. It's actually a leadership handbook for anyone, in any geographical location and in any industry, who wants to achieve remarkable results.

In describing Dubai's model in the following pages, I've decided to shy away, as much as possible, from using "traditional" leadership words and concepts like "visionary," "entrepreneurial," and "strategic." These are certainly relevant in Dubai's case; we all know that. Yet these overused words are devoid of meaning and fail to tell us what this leadership style is really all about.

Instead I chose to focus on twelve practical leadership habits, with each chapter homing in on a specific habit. Keep in mind this isn't an elective list where you get to pick and chose; this model requires all twelve habits be implemented together, in concert (to learn more about how I identified these habits, visit the About the Research section at the end of the book). Truth be told, practicing any one habit in isolation, outside of the context of the others, could be a formula for disaster. So remember: these habits only work when they're all blended together, like the ingredients to a recipe.

I must admit I'm impressed. I'm impressed with how Dubai created something out of nothing and has repeatedly come through very dark days to achieve success again and again. It was wholly counterintuitive for Dubai's early leaders to envision a luxurious city filled with pools, fountains, and skyscrapers when they didn't even have running water. It was implausible that they would build an infrastructure for the future when they didn't even have natural resources. And it was victorious that they were able to do so much more than their wealthier contemporaries. This is a real-life story happening right in front of our eyes, which we all need to understand. Dubai-style leadership is true leadership, the kind to have confidence in.

Sheikh Zayed bin Sultan Al Nahyan, the Founding Father and first president of the UAE, said, "He who does not know his past cannot make the best of his present and future, for it is from the past that we learn. If a man knows the past, he will, too, understand the present and will from that understand what lies ahead in the future."

To learn how to lead Dubai style, we need to walk the desert paths of the past in order to travel the glimmering superhighways of the future. For decades Dubai brought in—imported—leading minds from every field in order to learn from these experts. Now it's time for Dubai to teach *us*—to teach us how to lead!

THE "HABITS OF REMARKABLE SUCCESS" LEADERSHIP MODEL

KEEP THE FOCUS
WHERE YOU LOOK,
—THEY'LL LOOK—

ACT DECISIVELY &
—GIVE DIRECTION—

LEAD TODAY FOR
TOMORROW'S
—FUTURE—

MICRO-MONITOR
— WITHOUT —
MICROMANAGING

—— CREATE AN ——
ENVIRONMENT
WHERE OTHERS
—— SUCCEED ——

DUBAI'S STRATEGY

HAVE AN AMBITIOUS
—— APPETITE——

—DON'T ACCEPT—
"GOOD ENOUGH"
AS GOOD ENOUGH

STICK WITH THE
—— STRATEGY——

—— BE LOYAL ——
IN ORDER TO
GET LOYALTY

DEVELOP FUTURE
—LEADERS TODAY—

CONSULT TO BE
—INFORMED—
WHILE AVOIDING THE
CONSENSUS
LIMITATION

BE BRAVE
—TO MAXIMIZE—
A BUBBLE AND SPRINT
AWAY FROM CRISIS

| EXECUTION | STRATEGY | VISION |

ONE

Hello, Tomorrow

—Leadership Habit—
LEAD TODAY
FOR TOMORROW'S FUTURE

"Brothers, I think it is time for a new form of government," proposed Sheikh Maktoum bin Butti, speaking with the elders of the Bani Yas tribe in 1833.[8] The tribal leaders were huddled together in the then-desolate desert village of Abu Dhabi, today known as the ultramodern capital of the UAE.

Why a new form of government? people wondered, even though the tribe lived in near-primitive conditions. *What's wrong with our fatherly style?*

While historians differ on what was actually said by Sheikh Maktoum bin Butti that day (this shouldn't surprise us: Dubai is, after all, an oral culture),[9] there's no doubt that the Bani Yas had arrived at a dangerous crossroads. While widely regarded as one of the most prestigious and loyal tribes of Southern Arabia, they nonetheless found themselves under attack, both externally and domestically. The General

1

Maritime Treaty of 1820, which was in theory supposed to legitimize each new Ruler as the tribe's leader, was too new to provide the Bani Yas with any real safety and security.

At the time, two disparate types of government—really you could say two leadership approaches—dominated the Gulf. Today leadership experts call them the stick and the carrot. The stick—in the 1800s it was more like a "sword"—is leadership by inflicting the fear of punishment. Today, we would call these leaders dictators and possibly even a military regime. "Do what I say or else," order such leaders. It is understood that the "or else" is a mask for harsh punishment.

While the sword was relied on in other parts of Arabia, throughout most of its history the Bani Yas tribe had practiced the other leadership approach—the "carrot." This was a patriarchal, fatherly leadership style where the leader was like a "baba" taking care of the tribe.

To keep his power, a Bani Yas tribal chief was expected to take care of the tribe's every need—that is, "the carrot"—raising the children as future tribe members and a part of his extended family. He was tasked with maintaining the moral decency and welfare of the tribe, bringing honor to its relatives, and respectfully participating in family life. In effect, he was expected to be a good man as well as a strong leader.

This was patriarchal leadership in its finest form, which literally means "the rule of the father," who, as the chief of the tribe—the basic social unit of the time—was responsible for its well-being, reputation, and legal and moral property.

Now when people speak of patriarchy, it is void of the meaning it had in 1833. Society has given it an excluding connotation, referring to a social system where power is only held by "adult men." It's true that Arabia—well, we shouldn't single out Arabia, as a patriarchal style was prevalent around the world—was and still is male dominated. While the patriarch in nearly all cases was in fact male, our attention needs to stay fixated on the *obligations of the leader to the tribe*, rather than on gender. The chief's obligation was to care and provide for the tribe, just as both mothers and fathers contribute equally to raising healthy children, and employers provide support and sustainable success for their employees.

Confusing patriarchy and dictatorship is a grave mistake. The first relies on caring for the tribe as a footing of power. The other relies on fear, usually fear of the sword. One motivation—power—two different leadership approaches, the carrot and the stick.

What Sheikh Maktoum bin Butti had in mind was more, much more than the stick or carrot. He was compelled to do something different for his people. Something that would help them prosper.

SEEING TOMORROW

The Sheikh envisioned another form of government, an economic one that would permit the people to create businesses, have personal incomes, and accumulate wealth for their families. In other words, to live the "economic dream."

According to the whispers of history, he petitioned the elders, "I want our people to be able to produce and sell goods as the way we allocate resources in the tribe. We should lead for the future and build our people's ability to make their own living, provide financially for their families. We should think about tomorrow, today!" This was future-looking—you could say visionary—leadership.

In Dubai, leadership is about tomorrow. Actually in leadership-speak, "Hello, Tomorrow" is about seeing the future—a future that others don't. I'm not talking about uninspiring "vision statements" plastered on equally uninspiring company walls—posters that are walked past day after day without any acknowledgment.

What I'm speaking of is more than vision as espoused by management gurus. In Dubai, vision is seeing generations into the future and making decisions accordingly, even if those decisions incur short-term pain. It is more like a purpose, the reason for which you lead. This kind of leadership genius stands in sharp juxtaposition to that found in most publically traded companies and democratic environments. Both are pressured to achieve short-term results to prove their value to either shareholders or their electorate. Without having the surety of the long-term continuity of their vision, decisions are made for today, which can constrict future growth. Whereas in Dubai, decisions are made for tomorrow—a generation into the future. Later, we'll explore how Dubai's caring autocratic leadership system enables such pathfinding leadership to take place. (Yes, you read that correctly!)

Leading today for tomorrow's future is seeing what others may not see and going after what others may fear to do. For Sheikh Maktoum bin Butti it meant an invitation to create a new form of government—one based on economic approach—in order to provide for his people.

AN ECONOMIC FUTURE

I'll never know how Sheikh Maktoum bin Butti managed to have this flash of inspiration while living in the midst of the desert, practically cut off from the rest of the world. Surely, an economic future was a radical new approach. Although on the coast and open to the seas, Abu Dhabi was extremely isolated from the rise of industrial capitalism. It was very much a small tribal village and rural in its orientation, like much of the world at the time.

During the early summer of 1833, some nine hundred people from the Al Bu Falasah faction of the Bani Yas tribe prepared to travel to Dubai, presumably for its natural creek. Sheikh Maktoum bin Butti could have easily waited till the cooler desert winter to lead his people to Dubai. Instead the tribe's families packed their belongings on the backs of their donkeys and camels and carefully set out on foot. Today's mega-highway Sheikh Zayed Road didn't exist. What would today be a sixty-minute trip from Abu Dhabi to Dubai, on a thoroughfare that looks more like a supercar showroom, with its Porsches, Ferraris, and Range Rovers, took days, exhausting days. The tribe journeyed through the desert in sweltering summertime heat, eager to see what their leader was promising.

This historic migration was focused on tomorrow, a different form of government, an economic approach. This unusual mass migration would change the face of Dubai and over the generations even the trade routes of the world.

When the Al Bu Falasah tribe finally arrived in Dubai and joined the few hundred residents already eking out a living, they found a Dubai that was in need. Being just a fraction of the size of other port communities along the coast, it was barely known to the outside world. The influx of tribesmen and their livestock overwhelmed the existing infrastructure of Dubai and more than doubled the population.

The Al Maktoums quickly seized control, implementing a form of semi-governmental capitalism that began to put prosperity in the people's hands. They built a larger souq (the town's public market), added new services, and increased the town's fishing capacity. Merchants, craftsmen, and a better food supply soon flowed into Dubai. Still, this wasn't enough: even with the expansion of the souq, many of the craftsmen still had no shops. Instead, they squatted on vacant pieces of ground as close as possible to their customers. Clients seeking a specific service had to cry out: "Where is [for example] Hassan the tentmaker?"

Yet over the years, the sheikhdom prospered, and regional traders began to regularly visit the souq. During the 1830s, the annual indicator of economic success in the Trucial States was how many boats and men set out on the first day of pearling season for the six-month harvest. This was the barometer that validated Dubai's attractiveness and rising influence. And the oral records tell how Sheikh Maktoum watched with pride each year as more men and boats rowed from the shores, signaling Dubai's rising influence.

When Sheikh Hasher bin Maktoum, son of the founder of Dubai, took over in 1859, he focused on the same central theme—trade and commerce—as did his father. By this point, Sheikh Maktoum bin Butti's "vision"—the third form of government—was coming alive in Dubai. Without this focus, Dubai would have remained small, weak, and vulnerable. Instead it was growing. Never forgetting his father's leadership advice, Sheikh Hasher emerged as the most pro-business leader along the Trucial Coast. Unusual for a Gulf Ruling family at the time, the Al Maktoums kept company with business leaders to encourage their participation in Dubai's economy.

Compared with elsewhere, the people of Dubai lived well. As they began to enjoy economic success, they found that they were largely spared from the tribal infighting happening elsewhere in the Gulf. Somehow, the pro-business message had filtered through enemy lines, and Dubai escaped any further military conflict. (Of course, providing a stable place for British vessels to dock was a brilliant safeguard against attacks.)

One hundred forty years later, in the late 1980s, it seemed the economic form of government was firmly, permanently in place. When a group of expats approached Sheikh Mohammed bin Rashid (who later became Ruler of Dubai in 2006), saying that their corporations would help pay to make Dubai green, Sheikh Mohammed shot back, "Dubai will take care of those matters. You work hard, make money, and have a better life with your family. What is good for you is good for us."[10] In other words: let us take care of tomorrow so you can have economic success, today.

TOMORROW CAN BECOME ANYTHING

Today, "Hello, Tomorrow" has come to symbolize the vision of Dubai via the tagline of Dubai-grown Emirates Airline, the world's largest wide-body carrier. The airline's official slogan, "Hello Tomorrow," is about inspiring people to greet tomorrow's unlimited potential, now. "Hello" is a greeting, an invitation to a person, a place, or an experience. "Tomorrow" is a time, a place, a state of mind—the unlimited possibility of the future. The theme encapsulates life's potential by embracing the future with all its possibilities.

This slogan captures the essence of this leadership habit—invite people to join the unlimited possibilities of the future. You should see what's possible for your people even when they don't and lead them to make it a reality. Give your people hope for the future and they will follow you.

Tomorrow we can be anywhere, everywhere, and anything. I'm sure that Sheikh Maktoum bin Butti didn't envision all that tomorrow's tomorrow could mean in 1833, but he knew that leadership is about tomorrow. And the future is what every leader should focus on. This time-tested leadership habit passed from one generation to the next in Dubai and is still practiced today (as are all of the habits in *Leadership Dubai Style*).

Tomorrow is definitely what was on Majid Al Futtaim's agenda as he developed the 560-store Mall of the Emirates in the early 2000s, complete with its world-famous indoor ski resort. The site for Mall of the Emirates was in the middle of the desert, twenty-five kilometers away from central Dubai. It seemed like a long journey from town. Very little existed along the drive from Dubai to Abu Dhabi, except for the recently opened (April 2000) two-tower complex Emirates Towers, housing one of Dubai's few five-star hotels as well as the Ruler's office. The population and geographical spread of Dubai was a fraction of what it is today, literally a fraction—much less than half of what Dubai is today.

People just didn't understand. They pitied poor "Mr. Majid," as he's fondly known—he was going to lose the fortune he'd amassed from the hugely successful Deira City Centre shopping mall. *Why would he gamble away—throw away—all his money? Why build another mall?* It wasn't only the expats who questioned his sanity—neighbors and childhood friends did too.

Years later, after the mall became one of the Middle East's largest shopping, entertainment, and leisure centers, raking in $1,423 per square foot per annum (the seventh most profitable shopping center in the world),[11] I wanted to know how Mr. Majid kept focused and didn't get distracted by all his detractors.

Over *suhoor*, the meal eaten in the middle of the night during Ramadan, the holy month where Muslims fast from dawn to sunset, in his *majlis*,[12] I asked, "Mr. Majid, how did you stay focused when building Souq al Nakheel [now called Mall of the Emirates]?" And more interestingly, "How did you keep your people focused?" Like most nights during Ramadan, Mr. Majid's majlis was packed.[13]

In front of dozens of Emirati leaders, Mr. Majid paused and turned to the left to look at me. At this point, all sixty or so mainly Emiratis at the table went quiet. Mr. Majid turned his head back and stared deep ahead before responding.

"Can't you ask me about where we are going in the future?" he finally said. "That was so long ago." As the conversations at the table resumed, I looked down at my plate with a smile and thought, *While he didn't tell me what I wanted to hear, he did in fact just share the secret to staying focused — think about tomorrow.*

Although the mall was less than ten years old, he effectively reminded everyone there to stay focused on the future, which he clearly was. His ability to look a generation into the future was fortunate, as Dubai grew more in the next decade than most cities do in multiple generations. When it came time to expand the mall in 2010 and again in 2015, he was ready. It is rumored that he overbuilt the mall's infrastructure, so that at any point in the future he could easily expand it—a common practice in Dubai. While others were thinking about today, Majid Al Futtaim was leading for tomorrow—even though doing so came with a tremendous price tag.

Great leaders stay focused on the future even when the future isn't clear and when it isn't popular to do so. They aren't distracted by what's happening around them and what others are doing. Too often, too many so-called leaders—you know, the ones with positions of authority but who lack real foresight—spend their time reviewing yesterday when they should be delivering tomorrow. If you're doing a good job as a leader, there is very little you should be able to directly affect today.

Dubai struck oil in 1966, four decades before the Mall of the Emirates opened, with a surge of revenues following three years later in 1969. After laboring for years to build the economy and survivability of Dubai, Sheikh Rashid bin Saeed (Dubai's Ruler from 1958 to 1990) could have easily spent his "golden" years enjoying nature's blessing to Dubai. Instead he looked toward a long-term "tomorrow." Concerned that Dubai's oil would run out within a few generations, he famously said: "My grandfather rode a camel, my father rode a camel, I drive a Mercedes, my son drives a Land Rover, his son will drive a Land Rover, but his son will ride a camel."[14] So, he continued to invest (albeit a bigger sum after the discovery of oil) in the building of Dubai. He was mentally in the future, while physically in the present.

Sheikh Mohammed continues the tradition of "Hello, Tomorrow," today. "I do not know if I am a good leader, but I am a leader," he said shortly after being named Crown Prince in 1995. "And I have a vision. I look to the future, twenty, thirty years. I learned that from my father, Sheikh Rashid. He was the true Father of Dubai."[15] Like his predecessors, Sheikh Mohammed's mind is firmly set on the future. He is leading Dubai to a future that is far from today.

Leading today for tomorrow's future is seeing what others don't see, greeting what's possible for your country, business, or even your team. Have a clear purpose and give your people real hope for the future; if you do so, they *will* follow you.

Leadership isn't about today; it's Hello, Tomorrow!

When implementing "Hello, Tomorrow," keep in mind that this habit is the purest of visionary leadership. Don't water this point down by thinking of "vision" as it's traditionally espoused—a term totally devoid of meaning, due to its overuse. This leadership habit is "visionary" on the scale of Henry Ford and his Model T, Thomas Edison envisioning lightbulbs in every home, and Steve Jobs seeing the world's citizens using a device that combined a phone, an iPod, and an Internet communicator all in one. Not every one of your ideas has to be headline grabbing, but every moment you lead needs to be oriented toward the future.

In Dubai, "tomorrow" means what the rest of the world calls a "generation." It means a long-term perspective, never leading today—that is, for the short term. That is the fundamental shift involved in implementing this habit. Practically, this means adopting a timeline that conspicuously extends beyond what others would consider appropriate. Have the courage to take a longer view than others do in your industry. If they think five years into the future, then you should think ten years.

Dubai is evidence that long-term thinking leads to grand results.

TWO

Come One, Come All

——Leadership Habit——
CREATE AN ENVIRONMENT WHERE OTHERS CAN SUCCEED

E ven after living in Dubai for so many years, I still get chills when I drive down Sheikh Zayed Road, the main artery through the city. Not because of the unpredictable driving patterns, which are very interesting in and of themselves, a people from more than two hundred nationalities get behind their steering wheels and try to "dance" to their own "radio station." Talk about confusing! No, I get chills because nearly everyone who's living in Dubai is here because they can do better than they can in their home countries and maybe even anyplace else. Whether it's a busful of construction workers coming back from building the next skyscraper, a taxi driver carrying tourists across the city, or the CEO of a major business riding in his Bentley, all are living in Dubai because the city is contributing to their success—and they to its.

I admit I've become numb to the dizzying speed of development. And I take for granted the spectacular skyline, half of which was built before my own eyes. I accept the excitement and energy of the place as being normal. Yet, I still get chills because deep down I know Dubai is a special place where anyone and everyone can succeed.

When I think back to Dubai's formative years, I can only imagine what it must have been like to be one of the earliest expat businesses to set up "shop" on the shores of the city in 1901. Yes, you read that correctly—1901, not 2001, nor for that matter 1991. Dubai's strategy of welcoming others was put in place long before even the most tenured of today's expatriates immigrated here.

In 1901, Dubai was still a sparse coastal community and relatively unknown port outside of the local trading community. To the north were the ideally located twin ports of Sharjah and Ras Al Khaimah, home to the Qawasim tribe. The Qawasims were reputed as a "sea" tribe, enjoying much success on the open waters along the Persian coast, and as far away as the Indian subcontinent, controlling the regional waterways for much of the nineteenth century. They also controlled some of the shores and islands of Persia, including Lingah, the ideally located harbor city on the southern border of modern-day Iran. This made Lingah a major player in local trade.

At the end of the nineteenth century, the nationalist Persian government punished the Arabs, who were resented for their success and control of the Lingah port. Seemingly overnight the government hiked up import and export taxes, and slapped merchants who used the city souq with a fee. The merchants were outraged! Clearly the government wanted to displace them. Displace them they did!

CREATE THE RIGHT ENVIRONMENT

When this news traveled across the Arabian Sea (also known as the Persian Gulf), it set into motion the strategy that's still embraced today—welcome strangers, and do everything you can to foster their success. Taking advantage of Lingah's punitive actions, Sheikh Maktoum bin Hasher, Dubai's Ruler from 1894 to 1906, abolished most tariffs and reduced the few that remained, effectively establishing the idea of a "free zone" long before its time. This would set the stage for the city's future as a global commercial hub.

Sheikh Maktoum bin Hasher fully understood that if the largest merchant operators could be lured to Dubai, then those who traded closely with them would follow. Better than any other leader along the Coast of Oman, he acted on the opportunity trickling down from the historical shift in Lingah, dispatching an official envoy to sail the 173 nautical miles across the Gulf. Once there, the envoy was to persuade the most important merchants to relocate their businesses to Dubai. When those merchants eventually came, the Sheikh opened his arms, welcoming them to Dubai with a hearty *"Ahlan wa Sahlan!"* ("Welcome!")

Yet Dubai had to do something about its port, which was basically a casual fishing outpost masquerading as a commercial hub. The port wasn't nearly as appealing as the conveniently located ports of Umm Al Quwain or Ajman, or the large Qawasim-run ports of Ras Al Khaimah and Sharjah. So what did the Sheikh do? He committed to the strategy of "creating an environment where everyone can succeed." He offered free land on which to build, guaranteed tax breaks, and a favorable eye from the government. It was a clever move that has served Dubai well for ages. It was clear that Dubai was only interested in one thing: commerce. And the way to achieve it was through others' success.

Every vision—in this case, an economic form of government to people's prosperity—needs a strategy. Your purpose needs a way to come to life. For Dubai the strategy became "create an environment in which others can succeed," which practically meant Dubai would leverage its location and become a hub.

Shortly after setting this strategy in place, Dubai became a regular stopping point for ships as the principal commercial port in the Trucial States. Within a few years, Dubai's stature rose to the point where British commercial steamers began calling on the city every other week. The Port of Dubai significantly increased its trade with Persia, the Gulf countries, and India. Low tax rates (and in some cases no tax at all) attracted traders from all over the Gulf, as well as Indian merchants keen on financing the country's growing pearl industry. To drive this growth, Sheikh Maktoum bin Hasher turned Dubai into a near free-trade zone, which in turn boosted commercial activity and increased the city's revenues. This merchant activity eventually helped Dubai become the wealthiest emirate on the Trucial Coast.

Sheikh Maktoum bin Hasher knew that the only way to attract businesses and to keep them was to foster the correct environment. That attitude, which filtered down from the majlis, on through the government, ultimately became the mantra for Dubai. As we'll see in the coming pages, the port played a central role in the success of Dubai as the backbone of its strategy, and continued to grow progressively over the decades. Today, between Port Jebel Ali and Port Mina Rashid, Dubai has a combined capacity of 3.7 million TEU (twenty-foot equivalent unit, the standard unit describing a ship's carrying capacity). Dubai is now home to one of the top ten ports in the world. It is, in the truest sense, a global trade hub.

Sheikh Maktoum bin Hasher and every Ruler since did what every leader should do: create an environment in which others can succeed. Of course this made sense for Dubai economically, given its ability to use its geography as a hub. For you it makes sense because, as we'll see, it's the surest way to ensure your own future success.

HELP OTHERS SUCCEED

What did Dubai really have in 1901? Nothing more than a tiny port, which was inferior compared with other nearby ports. Though just a few kilometers away, the other ports were much better positioned in terms of proximity to Persia and making the turn through the Strait of Hormuz. So Dubai's leaders had to do something, something more than their competitors were already doing. They welcomed unhappy people from nearby tribes. They invited them to Dubai to increase their trade, to give them a shot at the good life.

Yet the only way these merchants would relocate to Dubai was if Dubai did something to help them. Earlier I pointed out that the government offered the merchants tax breaks and free land. What better way to entice them? Why wouldn't you choose a location where you could maximize your return, especially if you have to relocate anyhow? The cherry on top, for Dubai, was that it gained exactly what it wanted: a bump in commercial stature.

After arriving in Dubai, the merchant families took advantage of an autonomy that brought them economic and political power second only to the Ruling family. Over the years, the hundreds of Indians with British nationality who worked for Indian-British companies formed a new cadre of merchants. Many became wealthy to the point of constituting a significant economic class in Dubai. The Ruler and other leaders cheered for their success, as well as that of all the other citizens and residents. That is the role of leaders: to help others succeed.

I don't believe there's a more foundational thought about leadership than this—it is the leader's responsibility to support others to become more than ever before, more than they dared to dream of. No matter what the situation, a great leader's first response is always to think about the individual concerned—whether an employee, customer, citizen, boss, or investor—and how to help that individual experience success. What do leaders do? They help others succeed!

We learned more than a century ago that if times are tough where you live, come to Dubai, where you can succeed. Simply stated, this is the message of hope that Dubai radiates throughout the world: it is a place where you can come and succeed. Dubai is one place where it is understood that if all succeed, the vision will be realized; after all, the vision is putting people's prosperity in their own hands. This is true for all nationalities, economic levels, and walks of life. Helping someone else look good doesn't need to hurt you or make you look worse. In fact, when others' success is your priority, yours will be guaranteed to come. It's narcissistic leaders who struggle to understand how helping others succeed is beneficial to themselves.

We can learn from the example of Sheikh Saeed bin Maktoum (Ruler from 1912 to 1958). One morning, before anyone was awake, the Sheikh was walking through his modest home in Shindagha, the traditional center of Dubai, when he stumbled on one of the "palace" workers attempting to steal an expensive Persian carpet from the Ruler's majlis.

"Put it back," advised the Ruler. "The guards will certainly catch you."

Note that the Sheikh didn't call the guards, didn't fire the worker or even reprimand him. If the Sheikh turned the worker in, he would have been sent to prison. Instead he simply told the man to put the rug back. The thief took his advice and returned to work. Even in the midst of the complicated moment they shared, Sheikh Saeed was focused on the worker's success—his continuing on as a palace employee—rather than him losing his livelihood. And in return the Ruler got a very loyal employee who continued with him for years to come.

Contrary to self-centered thinking, leadership achievement can only become reality through others. You should earn your success based on your service to others, not at their expense. Leadership isn't an individual sport. Are you motivated to help others succeed? Even through difficult moments?

This is a mind-set transition that every leader has to internalize and implement. In their book *The Leadership Pipeline*, Ram Charan, Stephen Drotter, and James Noel mention this "shift" as one of three transitions a leader makes as he or she transitions from one leadership level to the next. (The others are the required leadership skills and how you allocate your time).[16] Early in your life and career, your success probably came from your individual achievement, what you did. At the end of a "good" day, what would you picture as your head hit the pillow? Your accomplishments, of course—"I closed that deal" or "I designed a new process," something that "I" (you) did. This is normal and expected, as society conditions you to think this way.

But as a leader—whether of a city, company, or team—you need to make the transition from "I" to "they"—"They grew our revenue" or "They created a new product," something that "They" (your team or company) did great. "They succeeded!" What's in it for you when you create an environment for your team to succeed? Your success, just as it was for Dubai.

YOU'RE (STILL) WELCOME HERE

In the same fashion that desperate miners descended on California in 1849 for the "Gold Rush," where gold nuggets were literally sitting atop the ground, Dubai experienced its own "rush" in the 1970s. In the wake of the oil boom, a slew of new projects dotted the landscape: schools, banks, hospitals, and hotels. The creek was deeper, the port bigger, and the airport was open. "Come here and you can succeed" proved to be an irresistible siren song: close to one thousand Asians a week were landing on the shores of the UAE. But there's one critical difference between the California Gold Rush and Dubai in the 1970s. In California, miners only had a precious commodity, not a welcoming environment. So, while a few did indeed walk away with millions in gold, most returned home empty-handed. In other words, they left without succeeding—abandoned, in a sense, by their leaders.

Expatriates in Dubai, however, were encouraged to stay and succeed. The "Rush" was in full force, but not only by those in the petrochemical industry. Every industry thrived—retail, property, tourism, financial services, and education, to name a few. A massive upward spiral of economic activity led to double-digit GDP growth. Think of it as an economic cyclone powering through Dubai for decades. The growth was so intense that if you built it, they *would* come.[17]

This ethos continued on through the decades. Rizwan Sajan, CEO of Danube, a billion-dollar building materials company in Dubai, recalls the welcoming environment he found in 1990.

"I was twenty-eight years old and forced to leave Kuwait, when Saddam Hussein invaded, where I had been working for the past ten years. Instead of returning to India, I decided to go to Dubai," Sajan proudly shared, sitting perched on his super-sized white leather chair. It was hard not to notice his ornate office and the Rolls-Royce parked outside—trophies of his success in Dubai.

Sajan asked his wife to give him six months to make a go of a new business, his own business—a building materials company. This was a big risk, given that previously, he was just a salesman in his uncle's company. He had never started a business, nor even managed one.

Sajan spent his life's savings of AED 100,000 ($27,000) renting an office and hiring a Pajero. ("A businessman couldn't be driving a Toyota Corolla," Sajan says.) His six months turned into twenty-five years, and Danube, the undisputed market leader in building materials in Dubai, is a billion-dollar business. How and why did this happen? Because Dubai welcomes and encourages others' success with its open-trade policies and government focus on supporting the private sector by reducing bureaucracy and creating stimuli for economic growth.

BE OPEN

Good jobs, a high standard of living, essentially guaranteed security, and a chance to succeed are the core reasons behind Dubai's global popularity. Just ask anyone living in Dubai, "Are you better off for being here?" Without fail, the answer is "Yes!" This is true for both locals and expats.

When I asked successful businesspeople in Dubai, "In your opinion, what is the secret, the essence, of leadership success in Dubai?" the answer was always "Openness!"

The perception of Dubai as an "open" city runs deep. Even in the 1960s, Sheikh Rashid was making an impression on others as an "open" leader, working as he did to maintain links outside his immediate circle. At both his office and his tight-knit majlis, he was open to others' ideas, in order to fully understand the scope of what could be created. Many of the ideas that shaped Dubai's development came from listening to the business community, talking with foreign governments, and observing what other cities were doing. Throughout the years, Sheikh Rashid maintained close links with the British, as well as the Indian merchants in his city. Much unlike the nineteenth-century leaders of Lingah, he understood that the merchants were important conduits in the process of development, and that they played active parts in their community.

Certainly, the presence of so many peoples began to threaten the native Emirati culture. Yet the Sheikh went out of his way to accommodate different faiths. In 1966, he donated land in the heart of Dubai to the Roman Catholic Mission, laying the foundation for what was to become St. Mary's Church (originally named Church of the Assumption). Over the next two decades the growing number of parishioners necessitated the demolition of the original building and the construction of a new and larger church (inaugurated in November 1989), with space to accommodate two thousand people.

Naturally these acts garnered a lot of controversy. Some native Dubaians were overjoyed by the acts, while others felt threatened, fearful that allowing "outside" ideas in would compromise their beliefs and way of life. The Sheikh, however, made it clear that intolerance wouldn't fly in Dubai, and would only cause friction.

When conflicts—an inevitable effect of a diverse population—started bubbling up between the Indian and Pakistani communities in Dubai, Sheikh Rashid shifted the focus to the collective identity. "Forget your nationalities," he ordered. "Dubai is home to both Pakistanis and Indians. . .I want each of you to consider yourselves esteemed guests of Dubai. But I have to warn you categorically that we will not allow foreign politics to be played out in the streets of the city."[18]

In other words, he drew the line on openness. Yes, you need to be open as a leader, but not to the point of division. Rather, use openness to pull together.

"Openness" here is more than the "boss" leaving his door "open" in order to encourage employees to stop by whenever they feel like it. It's truly accepting people, weaving them into the fabric of society. When recruiting Osman Sultan to become the founding CEO of du Telecom, Ahmed bin Byat told him, "I want you to look at this as part of the story of Dubai."[19] On a city- or country-wide level, accepting "outsiders," Dubai style, means opening up your community to a vast foreign influence and being okay with it. Dubai today is home to more nationalities than the United Nations has member countries. As noted before, nearly 90 percent of the population is composed of foreigners . . . 90 percent!

Yet before you get too kumbaya on the topic, keep in mind that openness is hard. Others aren't necessarily like you. I've heard several leaders casually complain about this, noting how easy it would be if everyone thought like they do. But they don't! Thus, you have to be open to their ideas and ways. Had there been a closed or semi-closed mind-set in Sheikh Rashid's majlis, Dubai today might be isolated and insignificant. Acceptance and tolerance are critical in creating an environment in which others can succeed.

This is especially true in Dubai's treatment of women. One day while Sheikh Mohammed was touring a government department (the Sheikh's visits are a subject we'll discuss in much more detail in "The Monitor" chapter), the director general told him that the HR department, led by a female director, decided to halt hiring women in favor of men, as women made up 70 percent of the workforce.

Pausing, before continuing with alarm in his voice, the Sheikh asked, "Are some of the women in your department performing poorly?"

"No!" the director general fired back. "And every woman applying to join us is more than qualified."

"Then hire every woman who meets your requirements," Sheikh Mohammed instructed. "And keep hiring them, even if women make up 100 percent of your workforce."

Partly because of the Sheikh's efforts, the percentage of female employees participating in the workforce quadrupled between 1980 and 1990, with the total number of national females working in all fields reaching 100,000 by 2010.[20] Emiratis continue to place a strong emphasis on traditional family and home values, but the government actively encourages women to enter the workforce as well.

Sheikh Mohammed says, "Dubai has moved beyond the phase of empowering women. Indeed, we are empowering society itself through its women; we are empowering our economy by strengthening the role of women."[21] The UAE ranks first out of 132 countries for "Women Treated with Respect" in the Social Progress Index (2014) conducted annually by the Social Progress Imperative, a Washington, DC-based nonprofit.[22]

The Ruler's message is loud and clear: "Beware men, lest women deprive you of all the leadership positions in the country!"

As one of many examples, Dubai chose its minister of state, Reem Al Hashimi, to lead Dubai's World EXPO 2020 bid committee. A graduate of Tufts and Harvard, and a former deputy chief of mission at the UAE Embassy in Washington, DC, Al Hashimi had proven her leadership knack again and again. When it came time to choose a formidable leader for one of Dubai's most ambitious pursuits, she was the one leading up the charge to convince the world that Dubai would be the ideal EXPO host—a continuation of the city's invitation to succeed.

Mariana Garcia Garza, a Mexican pilot living in Dubai, joins Al Hashimi in soaring to new heights and eagerly jumping on the bandwagon of success. Coming to Dubai after the collapse of Mexicana in 2010, she found a supportive environment that welcomed her to spread her wings. As a first officer at Emirates Airline, Garcia Garza is one of only two Mexican women to have flown the Airbus A380—the double-decker, wide-body superjet that is the world's largest plane.

Her path hasn't been easy. As a child, her ambitions were dismissed as childlike fancy. "I was determined from then on to become a pilot," she says. "Even in grade six, my teachers just thought it was cute—I wanted to fly like my dad." As a young pilot, she faced mix reactions. "In Mexico, people expected me to be at home looking after the kids, so it was challenging being a pilot," she said. "I would mostly get nice comments from other women who would say they were proud, and how it was so nice to have a woman flying the plane. But there were also guys who would say, 'If there's a woman flying, I'm not getting on.' You learn to live with it."[23] Now an experienced aviator, she is an inspiration to women, and is aiming to make history by becoming the first Mexican woman to captain the A380.

Reading through these examples, you may be infected by Dubai Fever. "I'll welcome everybody!" I can hear you excitedly proclaim. While creating an environment in which others can succeed is certainly admirable, you need to be mindful that it isn't at all costs. While you must be open to others' ideas and allow them to pursue goals that may be foreign to you, you must also preserve your identity and culture. As a leader, you need to be aware of the balance between your current culture and the benefits of openness. At any moment leaning too far in either direction can tip the scale, with potentially disastrous results.

Most importantly, openness shouldn't deter you from your strategy. Excessive openness is often misunderstood to mean letting anyone do what he or she might want. That isn't what this means at all Dubai or for you as a leader. Being open does mean allowing self-expression and even embracing uncomfortable ideas, but only as long as they further your strategy. You need to be open, but also aligned with your desired outcome.

Do you have a spirit of openness? Does your leadership contribute to others' success? Or does their success only contribute to yours?

Organizational hallways are littered with horror stories of "small-minded" bosses who put limits on how much success others are allowed to achieve. Don't be this person! Always think about how you can help your employees, team, and even company succeed. This became the core strategy, the business of Dubai.

Dubai's welcoming, even inviting, others to its shores highlights the admittedly challenging leadership habit of creating an environment in which others can succeed. Without this environment, you can rest assured that "Come One, Come All" would have been nothing more than an empty promise. Leaders exist to help others succeed. Every morning when you wake, you should be thinking about "them." And when you fall asleep at night, it should be with the satisfaction of how well "they" did. Rest assured: when you create an environment that helps others succeed, you'll succeed too.

THREE

The Hub

STICK WITH THE STRATEGY

On October 27, 2013, I was asked by Her Majesty's representative to Dubai, "Do you know what today is?" Sitting in his large yet starkly appointed office at the British Embassy, I stared out the window admiring the well-landscaped garden while pondering the date in my head. *October 27 . . . .* Seeing the distant look in my eyes, he jumped in. "It's the most strategically significant day in Dubai's history—today Al Maktoum Airport [at Dubai World Central] opens its doors to passengers."[24]

When it's completed, Dubai's master-planned economic zone Dubai World Central will be two times the size of Hong Kong Island and will house an estimated 900,000 people. This brand-new sliver of Dubai will be a multimodal logistics hub that seamlessly leverages its location next to Jebel Ali Port, connecting trade between sea and air. Al Maktoum Airport will add a future annual capacity of over 220 million passengers—to a city that's already home to the world's busiest international airport, Dubai International.

But I caught myself having a separate conversation in my head. *While this is an important event in the life of Dubai, what's really significant is that Dubai continued and continues to stick with its strategy.* Beginning with Sheikh Maktoum in 1901, leaders looked to leverage Dubai's location to create a hub: first an intra-Gulf hub, then a regional hub, and now an international hub. A hub where others could succeed.

Exactly one month later, the night that Dubai won the right to host EXPO 2020, I stood on the balcony of the Capital Club, Dubai's premiere private business club, talking with a group of journalists and businessmen about what EXPO 2020 would mean for Dubai. The anticipation was at a fever pitch as we held our breath waiting on the final decision. After the successful final vote was handed down, we watched celebratory fireworks explode over the Burj Khalifa, the world's tallest man-made structure. Suddenly the same thought from October 27 popped out of my mouth: "While tonight is significant, and we must applaud tonight's success, we mustn't ever forget where it came from. The DNA that led to us winning tonight was put in place over 110 years ago."

Immediately, I was challenged on my premise and even accused of over-romanticizing Dubai's heritage. To which I replied with what I consider to be a pillar of Dubai's leadership success: Dubai's strategy has remained intact ever since the days of the Lingah exodus. Today the strategy is just bigger, more sophisticated, and more impactful. At that point the journalists stopped what they were writing about and leaned closer, curious to learn more. The business leaders also expressed interest in learning the leadership habits behind Dubai.

CAPITALIZING ON THE CONNECTING POINT

As I brought the journalists and business leaders up to speed, I thought about another city that's deployed a similar strategy. At the same time the merchants of Lingah were packing up their belongings and heading over to Dubai in the early 1900s, New York City was rising to prominence as a connecting point—a hub, albeit by sea and rail. The growing United States economy in the late 1800s and early 1900s enticed millions of European migrants to leave their impoverished countries behind.

In search of an opportunity, countless numbers of immigrants endured crowded, unsanitary conditions near the bottom of steamships. Often they'd spend up to two straight weeks seasick in their bunks during the rough Atlantic crossing. Yet these same immigrants, who were in effect dehumanized by their journey to Ellis Island, infused the city with their labor and ideas. By the 1920s New York City was the largest city on the planet, and today remains the cultural and financial capital of the world. It became a hub for people looking for a new life.

While Dubai enjoyed a slightly different trajectory, in many ways its strategic model—that of being an interconnecting hub for a vast variety of people and things—emulates New York's.

In the early 1900s, Dubai quickly overtook Lingah's position as the southern Gulf's main pearl-trading center and distribution hub for imported goods. Under Sheikh Saeed's leadership and liberal trade policies, Dubai grew into a re-export hub for neighboring ports, capitalizing mainly on its prime asset: its natural ports. Goods that made their way into Dubai, either by sea or by land (often via camel), were subsequently re-exported and distributed to various settlements in the interior or smaller ports along the Gulf. With its "hub" infrastructure firmly in place, Dubai's reputation as a place that welcomed others' success further solidified in regional traders' minds.

From the beginning, Dubai had a clear strategy: become a commerce hub connecting people of all nationalities—including initially immigrants from Persia, the Subcontinent, and elsewhere in the Gulf—and then using it to help them succeed. And this is what Dubai continues to capitalize on.

STICK WITH THE STRATEGY

Sheikh Rashid understood the strategy that his grandfather had started—become a modern hub where others could succeed—and could see the potential for Dubai's future. In his first year of taking the reins—and while mourning the loss of his father—he boldly announced plans for a series of major projects. These would expand on the existing strategy by developing Dubai's infrastructure, while also preserving its status as a regional trading hub.

When Sheikh Rashid took over as Ruler in late 1958, Dubai had grown by leaps and bounds, yet still lagged behind in critical areas. Dubaians were dependent on distant wells and primitive natural pools of water for their everyday needs. Karama, outside the trading district of Dubai, was the largest of these pools. In winter rainwater would collect at Karama, and by summertime, this stagnant, fetid pool became a muddy hole in the ground, and a breeding ground for cholera. Transmitted mainly by drinking water, this small intestinal infection caused severe diarrhea and vomiting. Sheikh Rashid was painfully aware of the effects of cholera, having seen his father suffer through a severe spell of it in the 1930s. Generations of Dubaian families had been afflicted by this terrible disease.

His first priority was creating the Dubai Water Department, which (the Sheikh promised) would bring water to every home in Dubai. It would also elevate Dubai's water supply to World Health Organization standards, adding in needed aluminum, fluoride, iron, and silica. Dubai was surrounded by—but kilometers from—strong, fresh water wells. The Sheikh knew it was time to get that water into Dubai's homes, and to give people electricity. Once the Sheikh confirmed the wells' suitability, cement piping was laid across the growing city, supplying every home with fresh water. Within a few years, families started enjoying basic utilities, a change that utterly transformed their lifestyles.

Sheikh Rashid didn't stop there: in order to fulfill his strategy of Dubai being a major hub, the city needed a healthy creek. Its creek was its lifeline: a conduit for the majority of Dubai's trade. But the creek had begun to accumulate serious silt deposits, and the sandbars were causing larger vessels to get stuck, capsize, and—worst of all—sink. Only small dhows found the creek to be navigable. Anything larger was forced to anchor offshore and be unloaded onto transfer barges. And even the barges were getting stuck. As Sheikh Rashid knew, these circumstances wouldn't do. So, he launched a massive infrastructure project: the dredging and expansion of the creek.

Dubai's very existence and continued success depended on this project. Everyone—the merchants, community, and government—relied on the creek for their prosperity. Sheikh

Rashid knew that what was good for business, would be good for Dubai.

After announcing to his fellow citizens that they were dredging the creek and that within five years, every home would have running water and electricity, Sheikh Rashid said, "Let's build a bridge!" Can you imagine hearing those words when you don't even have running water or paved roads? Clearly, this was a leader who went *all in* in pursuit of his vision.

The building of the Al Maktoum Bridge would better integrate Bur Dubai and Deira, the two main sections of Dubai. Bur Dubai, on the west side of Dubai Creek, literally means "the mainland." On the same side of the creek is Shindagha, which was the early home of the Al Maktoums. Across the creek is Deira. While Bur Dubai was the government center, Deira was the commercial center. As Dubai continued to grow, it needed a more practical way to connect the two. The city needed infrastructure to make trade more practical. The common approach was to go down to the creek and jump on an *abra*—a small wooden boat, like a water taxi—to cross. Or to drive fourteen kilometers on unpaved sandy roads past what is today known as the Ras Al Khor Wildlife Sanctuary, a wetland reserve.

This wasn't acceptable!

In addition to establishing the Electric and Water Company, dredging the creek, and constructing the Al Maktoum Bridge, in that same year Sheikh Rashid announced the development of Dubai International Airport, and Dubai's first hotel—Airport Hotel, with eight rooms. Additional hospitals, schools and seaports, and the Middle East's tallest towers followed, in a frenzy of construction. Simultaneously, Sheikh

Rashid helped launch utility companies, banks, even a planning commission to aid with Dubai's rapid development. In other words: it was astonishing!

There was just one little problem in all this frenetic go-getting: Dubai didn't have any money to fund these projects. Its shoestring revenues came from trade and, to a smaller extent, oil exploration concessions. Any financial analyst would recommend that Dubai not borrow funds, and advise a lender not to lend to Dubai. Any one of these projects, let alone all of them, was an impossible investment, considering Dubai's limited and stretched resources.

Yet Sheikh Rashid took a risk, what some may call a reckless risk! He turned to the Emir of Kuwait for assistance in financing the dredging of the creek, borrowing an unheard-of £600,000. He also issued "creek bonds"—revenue derived from land reclamation made possible by the dredging. At the same time, he borrowed £190,000 for the two-lane Al Maktoum Bridge from Sheikh Ahmed bin Ali Al Thani, the Ruler of Qatar, who happened to be a close friend. (Coincidentally, his son later married Sheikh Rashid's eldest daughter, Mariam.) Of course, this was all in addition to the hundreds of thousands of pounds the city was pouring into the development of the airport, hospitals, and schools.

The development of the creek was a collective victory. With a bigger creek, more people did business in Dubai, businesses made more money, and Dubai was able to pay back its loan to the Emir of Kuwait early. Everyone succeeded!

Today, I listen to people express caution and concern about the pace of new projects being launched in Dubai. However, in 1959 the projects that Sheikh Rashid put into motion were sheer magnanimity. Very few homes had running water or electricity, and today's infrastructure wasn't in place—effectively, Dubai was still a dusty, remote sandy trading port with unpaved roads, making the simplest of tasks into an hours-long ordeal. Because of Sheikh Rashid's vision for the future, we now enjoy the core of the infrastructure we could so easily take for granted. This super-sized ambition is what you need to emulate if you want to achieve grand results.

Sheikh Rashid's momentous 1959 brings together what we have learned thus far: that leaders, at least Dubai-style leaders, *do*. These leaders act for tomorrow, today. They create an environment in which others can succeed. And, perhaps most importantly, they stick with the strategy, believing that success begets success. Sheikh Rashid was insistent that Dubai would become what his grandfather said it would become.

AVOID STRATEGY TEMPTATIONS

Sheikh Rashid's expansion of the infrastructure in the 1960s teaches us the value of adhering to a preexisting strategy. Yet many modern theorists, in an effort to persuade us that they're propagating "long-term thinking," have tricked us into believing that "real" strategies only last a few years. When a new monarch or president takes over, it's fashionable to replace all his or her previous ministers and lieutenants, which invariably results in a change of direction. The same goes for new CEOs, or simply team leaders, who often want to make their mark by ditching the previous strategy and starting from scratch again. This is the default setting—often these leaders don't even examine the soundness of the existing plan.

In Dubai the commitment is the antithesis of what is practiced in many boardrooms, where boards change direction every three years whether it's needed or not. This is a long-term strategy, looking generations into the future.

A change only makes sense when there's a proven flaw in the existing strategy or external realities dictate such. Too often, the real fatal flaw is failing to stick with the preexisting strategy. Changing strategy doesn't rectify the execution challenge: it just resets the strategic clock and buys time. Crafting a new strategy can actually become a "strategic" distraction.

Even worse is the management mistake that confuses "strategy" with a budgeting exercise or annual planning meeting. I see far too many companies host what's called a "Strategy Retreat," only to spend the whole time setting budgets and plans for the upcoming year. Rather than modeling what we learn from a century of Rulers in Dubai who focused on delivering the plan and expanding it at every opportunity possible, all while keeping the core, long-term strategy in place.

Many people argue that you need to change your strategy based upon external environments, changes in market conditions, and what your competition does. At times—less frequently than what's practiced in reality—you may need to do so. When you're tempted to change directions, ask yourself: "Am I doing this because my strategy has failed or because of a need driven from the external environment?" Perhaps it's really the execution of the strategy that failed. It's easy to think you need a new strategy, when all you might actually need are new ideas on how to implement your existing one.

In Dubai's case, even as times radically changed, leaders always stuck with the same strategy. (The introduction of industrial capitalism, the advent of air travel, and the emergence of computer technology all occurred during the city's lifetime.) Of course, the strategy's been tweaked, but the overall essence remains the same: giving people economic independence, creating an environment in which others can succeed, and be a hub, albeit with a much broader geographical reach. Dubai's success is the result of the natural progression of an existing strategy, not an abrupt change.

SAME STRATEGY, ONLY GRANDER

In 1959, long before understanding all that the rise of passenger air travel would signify, Sheikh Rashid knew that an airport was central to the continuation of Dubai's strategy. Boeing's first jet airliner, the 707, had replaced the Douglas DC-4 and DC-7, making jet travel commercially successful. Pan Am, with its Hollywood depiction of posh air travel and its modern fleet, had made air travel aspirational for everyone. The "jet age" was something magical and marvelous. Riding in an airplane made everyone feel like a movie star. And all of a sudden anyone could.

Sheikh Rashid watched these developments closely, knowing that in order to be a world player, Dubai had to be part of this newly connected, glamorous world of travel. Yet the city remained painfully isolated: the nearest airport was in the emirate of Sharjah, which then was often a whole day's travel away. When pressure rained down on the Sheikh from members of the merchant community, who offered to help pay for the airport, he knew it was time to take action. When Dubai decided to build out its port and become an intra-Gulf competitor, the 1960s were really just like 1901 all over again.

In 1960 the Sheikh opened Dubai Airport to remain competitive and—hopefully—to become a global hub. Dubai simply couldn't be dependent on someone else. When tiny Dubai

Airport opened, it had just one runway—an 1,800-meter airstrip of compacted sand that was only able to handle aircraft the size of a Douglas DC-3s. But it was a start. The first year, two airlines—Middle East Airlines and BOAC (which eventually morphed into British Airways)—flew to and from Dubai, with the British assuming control of operations. Three years later, an asphalt runway was constructed, allowing Dubai to receive its first "big" jets.

Even while building the airport, which was obviously future oriented, Sheikh Rashid overbuilt, thinking a generation ahead of time. He constructed a five-hundred-spot car park next to the airport—an absurdity, considering that there weren't even five hundred cars in Dubai at the time. "Dubai's streets aren't even paved!" people grumbled. "There aren't even five hundred cars in Dubai!" For a few years the car park did, in fact, sit virtually unused. But within five years, the airport and its car park were at capacity, needing to be expanded. By the end of the decade, Dubai Airport welcomed nine airlines serving some twenty destinations.

As noted earlier, overbuilding is a common practice in Dubai. Rather than being confined by today's needs, most major assets are built with an infrastructure to support future expansion, which adds costs that you would normally skimp on if you weren't leading for the future. Would you ever do this while being pressured for near-term financial results, as Wall Street does?

What happened in the next few years highlights the essence of what has become leadership, Dubai style. Rather than giving preference to any one airline, Dubai adopted open-sky provisions that effectively embraced free-market competition, giving all airlines an opportunity to compete, to succeed in

Dubai. I have to wonder if Sheikh Rashid was secretly thinking that his sons would see Dubai become a global hub and was looking way into the future, far ahead of his time.

Thanks to Sheikh Rashid's foresight and determination, a second gateway, a door, had opened into the city, giving Dubai another entry point into the world. What just years prior were distant cities, taking weeks to access via boat or land, became easily accessible destinations located just hours away. The steady climb in passenger travel connected far-flung, previously isolated people and parts of the world. From its humble beginnings, Dubai Airport grew to become one of the busiest airports in the world, eventually taking the top spot from London's Heathrow in terms of international passenger traffic in 2014.

Perhaps the main lesson we can learn from Sheikh Rashid's rule is to stick with it—the strategy! If your existing one is sound, resist the constant temptation to continually craft a new strategy, if your existing one is sound.

A STRATEGY FOR TOMORROW

Because of Dubai's insistence in sticking with the original strategy, thousands of families today have an opportunity to come to the city and succeed. Not at all unlike the tribe that packed up its goods onto a caravan of camels in 1833, or the merchants who sailed up the Trucial Coast in 1901, families from around the world today stuff entire households in shipping containers, making their way to Dubai by jumbo jet. While the journey is a far simpler trip by air, Dubai's new residents are still taking a fundamental leap of faith, embracing the concept of "Hello, Tomorrow" and staking their hopes on a place that will support their success.

In 1901, when Dubai welcomed the merchants from Lingah, what Sheikh Maktoum bin Hasher was essentially doing was listening to foreign merchants and answering, "What will help you succeed?" He learned what they wanted from a home port and the conditions that would attract more traders to Dubai—protection by a government against rising taxes. He then shaped his plans accordingly. In addition to the habit of sticking with the strategy, the Rulers after him also continued the practice of listening: listening to understand what the merchants wanted, and making it easy for them to do business.

Dubai's location is definitely important. But what's more important is the attitude of its leaders, which is what you can emulate. Leaders should be obsessed with making others' work as easy as possible, and with removing all the unnecessary steps in order to successfully do business.

Dr. Amina Al Rustamani, CEO of TECOM, the operator of many of Dubai's leading business parks and free zones, is a modern-day example of practicing exactly what Sheikh Maktoum bin Hasher did over a century ago. She listens! In 2013, while building TECOM's newest free-zone business park, a fashion, design, and luxury hub called Dubai Design District (or "d3" as it's known), she and her team wanted to hear from the community. The thousands of artists, fashion designers, and creative minds across the region had expressed a desperate need for a real, living community, so it was important that Al Rustamani get the execution right.

"I listened to the design community to understand what would help them succeed," she told me.[25] By listening to the "merchants," Al Rustamani's team was able to continue the strategy of Dubai—to be a place where others can succeed.

One of those modern-day merchants was Zayan Ghandour, founder of fashion boutique S*uce. Says Ghandour, "I would never have been able to do what I've done if it wasn't for that Dubai conviction that anybody can start a business and succeed. There is a beautiful energy and spirit that encourages entrepreneurship, allowing people to believe in their dreams and work hard to make them happen."[26]

TECOM is wonderful illustration of Dubai sticking with its strategy. As we just saw, Dr. Amina listens to the "merchants" just as the leaders who came before her did. The very business model of the free zones is today's equivalent of inviting the traders from Lingah to Dubai. The primary difference is that Dubai now invites the whole world to bring its business here. More than a century after the merchants of Lingah arrived, the strategy remains the same.

Recognizing again that Dubai's success is dependent on shaping the future, in December 2012, Sheikh Mohammed invited eighty prominent business leaders, both expat and Emirati, to strategize about Dubai's future. Well, with Sheikh Mohammed it was more than strategizing—it was about uncovering realistic ideas to put into action. This was a version of his practice from the 1980s, when he would invite sixty to seventy leaders to Za'abeel Palace to have a lively debate about the future of Dubai. He would ask them, "What can we do to make Dubai better?" This was a direct challenge to the leaders in Dubai to think about the future and continue the essence of its strategy: helping others to succeed.

It would have been easy for Sheikh Mohammed to sit back and enjoy the spoils of Dubai's remarkable successes over the past decade. By 2012, the Burj Khalifa was open, Dubai's metro was succeeding, and scores of people from around the world were traveling to Dubai both for pleasure and business. But he chose to follow the example set earlier: In times of success, work harder to prepare for tomorrow. Make sure the environment in which others can succeed gets even better and flourishes.

Was he thinking of changing Dubai's strategy? No! Neither was he content with the present. He was looking for ideas on how to do things better, given the changing market conditions.

The leaders present at this brainstorming event came from diverse backgrounds—they were Emirati, Lebanese, British, Indian, and several other nationalities. They also had different experiences and embodied every industry important to Dubai—retail, hospitality, advertising, travel, industrial, property development, financial services, construction, and the major government entities. Each leader was assigned to a table of eight. Many of the leaders knew one another, yet some knew one another only by reputation.

After everyone was seated, envelopes were handed out to all the tables. In each was a specific "opportunity"—a scenario residing outside the participants' day jobs, to which they were to answer: "How can Dubai add greater value?" An example of the scenarios includes:

An Emirati family with six children. A retired couple living in the UK. A second-generation NRI [non-resident Indian] family. Some even peered inside a company's perspective: *A multinational company with its regional HQ in Dubai.*

While these scenarios may seem vague, they accurately represented the constituents, customers, and residents of Dubai. People for whom Sheikh Mohammed wanted to ensure Dubai continued to add value.

As various ideas were presented, Sheikh Mohammed encouraged everyone to continue talking, even if he disagreed with what they were presenting. He was open to what others had to say and how they thought Dubai could create an even better environment for others. Of course, he knew and accepted that many of the ideas would also benefit the carrier of the idea. But that wasn't a problem; Dubai has long been an environment of mutual success, and "ahead-of-its-time" ideas.

While ideas did emerge from that day—such as for the tourism sector to focus on families, global events and attractions, and Dubai's status as a business destination. More so that day shaped everyone's behavior to keep thinking about the future. In my interviews, attendees repeatedly shared this as an example as to how Sheikh Mohammed keeps the focus on the strategy for the future.

From a leadership point of view, the "romanticized" concept here isn't the strategy that Sheikh Maktoum bin Hasher instituted in 1901. It is the fact that the strategy is still followed today. It is remarkable and attention grabbing when a vision and strategy pass from one leader to the next—let alone over the course of a century through six different leadership eras.

As a leadership specialist, this kind of "sticking with the strategy" stops me in my tracks. As mentioned before, in most organizations, when a new leader takes over, he or she tosses out the previous leader's plans and tries to make his or her "mark." The temptation is to succumb to "market conditions" and try something new and different, perhaps as a way to gain praise or "credibility." But in Dubai, the successors resist this "ego trip" and try to stay true to the fundamentals of the preexisting strategy. When you have a compelling purpose as the core of your strategy, that strategy has the potential to last decades, generations, and even centuries into the future. Find your purpose, implement your strategy, and stick with it.

Sticking with the strategy is one of the more contrarian habits, but a century of adherence highlights its value. Being able to build this leadership habit is highly dependent on your ability to ward off temptation—to not succumb to the urge to try something different. In this era of "innovation," it's understandable why you'd want to change course. But "innovation" begs the question, "What are you innovating for?" The answer is: fulfilling your strategy, not ditching it entirely.

As a young boy, I was taught, "Don't give up!" with the explanation that people often do so right when they are on the verge of achieving the desired result. The opportunities ahead of you are usually much larger than you initially anticipated, and so is the required effort you have to put in to realize them. So be persistent, patient, and do not stop in the middle of the road.

This simple yet powerful advice forms the heart of this leadership habit. Stick with your strategy; never give up on the original vision.

FOUR

Hunger of Need

HAVE AN AMBITIOUS APPETITE

After watching the idling car sitting for hours near Dubai International Airport, the police officer finally tapped on the driver's side window.

"Is everything okay in there?" he asked. The car's engine was running and the windows were fogged up, raising all sorts of suspicion. The air conditioning was on full blast to combat the hot, humid summer night.

"Um, sure officer," the young man inside, Hadi, answered after the tap on the window woke him from a deep sleep. Thinking quickly on his feet he added, "My friend's flight is delayed and I live too far from here to drive home and back."

Fortunately for Hadi, the officer accepted his explanation.

But there was no friend whose flight was delayed. And Hadi didn't live a long way from the airport. Actually, he didn't live anywhere. Hadi had turned his rental car into a makeshift hotel.

A few days earlier, with just two hundred dollars in his pocket—his entire life savings—Hadi moved to Dubai for a new job. But he had no place to stay and didn't have enough money to rent an apartment or stay in a hotel room, even the cheapest of them. So he rented a car and made it his "hotel" for his first week in Dubai, bathing at a petrol station in between driving to and from work.

What would make someone like Hadi risk everything? Do the unheard of—sleep in a car for five nights?

The answer is that Hadi had too much to lose, not to lose. He had a hunger of need. Back home there were no jobs, no opportunities, no hope. His back was up against the wall. Today he's a partner in a growing business in Dubai and is succeeding beyond his wildest dreams.

We've learned in the previous chapters that Dubai welcomes people like Hadi to succeed. But Dubai itself is a lot like the "Hadis" who have come here in pursuit of a better future, ambitious to achieve something. Dubai started with its own "hunger of need" when Sheikh Maktoum bin Butti led his tribe on the strenuous journey through the desert in 1833. The people who became Dubai's leaders craved something more; they wanted to help people to have personal incomes, to have the best life possible. It was a "burning bridge" moment. There would be no returning to the way life was before. There was no choice in the early days but to succeed in order to survive.

Dubai's history is marked by a hunger of need, not of want. A hunger of need is when you have to do something; you can't live without it. This need to survive drove Dubai's early ambitions. A want, on the other hand, is something that is nice to have. You don't really have to have it, but you "crave" it. As we will see later in this chapter, for Dubai the "want" is actually a habit that was built from a hunger of need.

HUNGRY TO SURVIVE

Sitting in his office reminiscing about the history of Dubai, Emirati businessman Dr. Ahmed Hassan Al Shaikh shared, "The early period was a tough time. It created the 'it must be done' mentality. There was no choice. Later this choice became a challenge to do more. Survival turned into a habit to do more." He grew up in the era of transition and went "from a hunger of need to a hunger of habit."[27]

Prior to the discovery of oil, Dubai built its infrastructure merely for survival, not for its admiration, doing so with borrowed funds. The discovery of oil was tempered by Sheikh Rashid's farsighted—and in all likelihood accurate—realization that the oil would run out. "I have good news and bad news," he said at the time, in 1966. "We found oil, but not much." So again there was a hunger of need: Dubai had to use its oil funds to build an economy that wasn't oil dependent. Notably, Dubai's oil wealth was used to fund the existing strategy instead of making oil itself the strategy.

When you're hungry, you naturally become obsessed with satisfying that hunger. This type of hunger is what fuels Dubai-style ambition.

Sheikh Mohammed opens his book, *My Vision*, with the following well-known saying highlighting the hunger of need in Dubai-style leadership:

"With each new day in Africa, a gazelle wakes up knowing he must outrun the fastest lion or perish. At the same time, a lion stirs and stretches, knowing he must outrun the fastest gazelle or starve. It is no different for the human race. Whether you consider yourself a gazelle or a lion, you simply have to run faster than others to survive."[28] [29]

Let's get right to the point: in order to achieve something big, you have to have big ambition, whether it's driven by survival or want. You have to desire something so much that you strive for it with focused urgency. When you're faced with the need to survive, it's easy to strive to stay alive. As we'll see in this leadership habit, ambition is the fuel for leading Dubai style.

SEEING WHAT OTHERS DON'T

As Dubai began to accumulate wealth, Sheikh Rashid famously said, "[W]hat is the point of keeping it in the bank? I'm looking ahead perhaps fifty years. We've got money, so what is the point of keeping it in the bank? Eventually we will need more capacity, and then it could cost us double or triple the price to build it."[30] He wisely stretched Dubai's present revenues as much as he could, "today," to avoid getting gouged, tomorrow.

Keeping with the hub strategy, in 1976, Sheikh Rashid chose to invest Dubai's new wealth in building yet another—a third—port. His advisers, mainly merchants based around the traditional trading areas of Deira and Bur Dubai, wished he would reconsider, or at least delay. At the time, Mina Rashid,

Dubai's second port, was being expanded. So why a new port? And why in Jebel Ali, an undeveloped stretch of coastline far from the central business district? It was literally in the middle of nowhere.

A number of businessmen went to Sheikh Mohammed, Sheikh Rashid's son, trying to get him to talk his father out of proceeding. "You know that you have special standing with your father and that he listens to you," a community representative said. "Your father wants to build a new port at Jebel Ali. We beg you to tell him that we already have a big port at Port Rashid—it is adequate. The country is suffering from stagnation, and the new port will lead to overcapacity and losses."

When a suitable opportunity came up, Sheikh Mohammed told his father what the businessmen said. Puffing on his pipe, Sheikh Rashid said, "Oh Mohammed, I am building this port now because there will come a time when you won't be able to afford it."

The argument was settled, and what is arguably one of Dubai's most valuable commercial asset was born. The Jebel Ali Port and surrounding Free Zone (today one of the biggest free zones in the world) contributes significantly more to Dubai's GDP than oil does. Sheikh Mohammed shares, "My father was the first to think of this project. If the project had been suggested to consultants or subjected to an economic feasibility study, it would never have been implemented."[31] This stroke of genius highlights what leaders are to do—take risks.

BUILDING A HUNGER OF HABIT

For the sons of Sheikh Rashid—Maktoum, Hamdan, Mohammed, Ahmed—even his youngest brother, Ahmed bin Saeed, whom he raised as a son, Dubai's hunger of need became a hunger of habit. By the time they took over the leadership of Dubai in 1990, the "era of need" was history. It was clear Dubai was going to survive. But the sons wanted more for Dubai; they were still hungry. This move from doing something because you have to in order to survive, to doing it because it is now part of your DNA is what I call "the hunger of habit." A habit is what you do because it is now natural.

It's quite difficult to create hunger in someone—I mean aside from without withholding food. So, how did the sons of Rashid learn to be hungry as leaders?

They became hungry—you could even say starving with ambition—by having an up close and personal seat to the Father of Dubai. They witnessed their father pursue the future with the intensity of a famished man chasing after his next meal. Not just a meal for him, but food to feed his family for generations to come. They watched as their father rose before dawn to participate in Fajr prayers (the first of five daily prayers in Islam), and then jumped into his truck to make his daily inspection tour of Dubai—seeing for himself the projects that were underway. ("The Monitor" chapter will examine this specific tactic.) Following breakfast they would see him head to his morning majlis to manage the affairs of his rapidly growing city. His hectic days would end only many hours later, after the conclusion of the evening majlis, on many nights after midnight.

Sheikh Rashid took very seriously his sons' preparation as leaders. He was actively involved in the boys' training and development, knowing the responsibilities that were going to be thrust on their shoulders at a young age.[32] He recognized the need to ensure that his sons would later lead in a way that was harmonious with his own vision for Dubai. In addition to their formal studies, the boys often participated in the majlis, both their grandfather's and their father's, listening to stories and anecdotes about Dubai's heritage, and interacting with local businessmen and meeting visiting heads of state. I can almost hear the conversation around the family table: "Boys, we are going to get running water to every house in Dubai. Boys, we are going to build an airport. Boys, . . ." This was the traditional way of passing forward the city's history from one generation to the next.

No wonder Sheikh Mohammed, the present Ruler, doesn't shy away from ambitious plans and is comfortable launching multiple projects at a time. He grew up in a home where shooting for the moon was, quite simply, par for the course.

ADDICTED TO ACHIEVEMENT

When the federation of the United Arab Emirates was formed in 1971, each son took a leading role at the federal level. At the age of twenty-eight, Sheikh Maktoum became prime minister; at twenty-five, Sheikh Hamdan became finance minister; and at twenty-one Sheikh Mohammed became defense minister. They were the youngest people in the world to be serving in their respective positions. Dubai, even the UAE, was still in the era of "need." Of course, oil wealth was now a reality, but this was still a fledgling nation coping with the impending British withdrawal and the reality that Iran might consequently see them as vulnerable.

I've tried to imagine what it would have been like to go from being teenagers in a small city of twenty thousand people, with no running water, electricity, paved roads, or local banks, to being thrust into the top leadership roles of a brand-new nation of 272,000 people—and, decades later, to lead a metropolis of over two million residents and a country of nine million. But I can't. It's practically unfathomable to imagine the urban metamorphosis they witnessed, at the toil of their hands. This sort of "miracle" simply can't happen without ambition.

When you're hungry for so long, it becomes your habit. The desire to achieve is addictive. When huge ambition is the common, everyday way of thinking around you it naturally becomes your own habit. Seeing the biggest, tallest, and fastest being erected around you, you feel left out if you can't yourself lay claim to a super accolade. After being in this environment for a while, *not* thinking big seems odd. Operating without a fear of the size of an idea is the essence of this leadership habit.

This kind of thinking fosters a competitive environment, in which big bets are the norm. In Sheikh Mohammed's case, this competitive spirit has spilled over to horse racing. To improve his odds of winning, Sheikh Mohammed is known to run multiple horses in the same race. He can't predict which horse and jockey will deliver on race day, so he creates options to improve his odds of winning. Not only that, but his brothers often have horses in the same races. Mirza Al Sayegh, an accomplished horseman, made me laugh when he quoted the Sheikhs: "I don't compete against my brothers! But my trainers do. I did not get the horses to stay in the stable."[33]

This approach leverages natural tensions and conflicts—consider Emirates Airline and its "competitor," the low-cost carrier flydubai. Each is owned by the government of Dubai, yet they compete, serving several of the same markets. Similarly, during the 2000s, Sheikh Mohammed did not "bet" on any one person, instead appointing Sultan Bin Sulayem, Mohammed Al Gergawi, and Mohammed Alabbar to each lead one of Dubai's major development and holding companies. Rather than merging these entities together, he opted to keep this "trinity" of chairmen (as they were referred to) separate. This created internal competition to be the best and kept each on their toes.

Combining ambition with a need, a real hunger, certainly arouses action. When you're hungry, really wanting something, you're willing to do whatever it takes to get it. This hunger is uncommon generally, but ever present in Dubai. In order to achieve, you need both the wanting and the willingness. This alchemy between hunger and ambition is what Dubai-style leaders are all about. The question is: Are you hungry enough to achieve grand results? To achieve what others are afraid to even talk about?

TAKING RISKS

By 1984, Dubai Airport was still growing so quickly that leaders decided to ask Bahrain-based Gulf Air, the darling of the GCC region, to increase the number of flights to the city. Somehow, demand for seats still outstripped supply, despite the region's economic woes and the ongoing Iran-Iraq War. Given that Dubai was already Gulf Air's most profitable center, and the airline operated more flights to Dubai than any other destination, leaders thought for sure the answer would be "Yes, absolutely!"

Instead they received a resounding "No!" In fact, Gulf

Air threatened to drastically *drop* the number of flights into the city, which would cause Dubai to lose valuable capacity. Gulf Air was unhappy with Dubai's "open skies" policy, which essentially gave all airlines a fair and equal shake; in other words, a place where others could succeed. Faced with increased competition from carriers around the world, including Cathay Pacific and Singapore Airlines, and specifically competition in Pakistan, which was limiting Gulf Air's landing rights in Northern Pakistan, Gulf Air aggressively lobbied Dubai for protection, and for restrictions to be placed on other airlines. Gulf Air's message was clear: they wanted to have a hand in shaping Dubai's aviation strategy, and in turn to rule the skies.

Gulf Air's move wasn't to be ignored, nor were Dubai's leaders about to give in to the airline's demands. Leaders faced an impasse: Should they stick with their original strategy of welcoming everyone—"open skies"—or give in to Gulf Air, possibly negatively affecting the economy? The real question was: Should Dubai stick with its century-old strategy of creating an environment in which others can succeed, or allow just one airline the opportunity to do so?

Dubai wouldn't do it. Dubai is a place that allows others to come and succeed, even when it creates competition.

"I was in the InterContinental Hotel one afternoon in late 1984 and [was] paged to answer the telephone," recalls Sir Maurice Flanagan, director and general manager of airport service company DNATA which handled cargo and general sales for all airlines, including Gulf Air. On the line was Sheikh Mohammed, then-UAE minister of defense and in charge of civil aviation.

"When did you say was the date on which we should

launch an airline?" His Highness asked. Flanagan never figured out how Sheikh Mohammed knew he was at the Intercontinental having coffee.

"October 25, sir," Flanagan said, referencing the release date of autumn/winter schedules. There had been talk about Dubai starting its own airline, but the general sentiment was that Gulf Air would back down, as their position was financially unsound.

"Thank you," replied Sheikh Mohammed. And abruptly the line went dead.

Then came March 25, 1985—the day Gulf Air acted on its threats and dropped the number of weekly flights to just thirty-nine, from eighty-four.

Days later, Flanagan was summoned to Za'abeel Palace. "I've looked closely at your proposal for an airline," said Sheikh Mohammed. "How much money do you need?"

"$10 million," Flanagan said, "although others were talking of $40 million or $50 million." Ten seemed like a nice, safe Maktoum sort of number!

"Here's a check for $10 million. Tomorrow an account will be opened with the National Bank of Dubai where this can be deposited. Now, don't come back and ask for any more money. You must operate without any government subsidies. Don't expect protection from competition because you will have no protection." From year one, Emirates Airline had to be profitable.

Sheikh Mohammed asked again, "When is the next appropriate date on which we can launch?"

"October 25!" said Flanagan.

"That is when we should begin," said Sheikh Mohammed. With only six months' notice, Flanagan was to launch

Emirates Airline. The meeting was over.

Instead of giving in to Gulf Air's threat, Dubai's leaders took a far bigger risk, which would prove to be much more profitable in the years to come. A hunger of need makes you do what you might not have done otherwise. Painful but satisfying, hunger "pangs" drive you to find food where before you might not have looked. When you are starved, your ambition drives you.

Flanagan, along with a ten-person team, put the business plan into action with no protection against competition in the airline's home market, and no subsidies of any kind. Dubai didn't budge on its strategy for Gulf Air and wasn't about to make an exception for Emirates Airline either.

Starting an airline in the midst of a regional war, shaky economic conditions, and on a shoestring budget in a narrow-margin competitive industry only comes only from a true hunger, real ambition. When you're hungry, you're willing to do what a satisfied person deems unreasonable and impossible. What is perceived as risky outside of Dubai and holds others back isn't so here.

Emirates Airline started with two aircraft leased from Pakistan International Airlines; after three or four profitable years, they were in a position to buy their own planes. Thirty years later, Emirates is one of the largest airlines in the world, serving more than 130 destinations worldwide. Does Emirates Airline still have a hunger of need? The answer is that their hunger of need has transformed into a hunger of habit, which we will discuss in more detail shortly.

Ambitious leaders take risks. They are obsessed with their strategy and are willing to do anything, within the boundaries of the law and their ethics, to make it happen. When a leader is hungry he or she has a big risk appetite, making you risk more than others think wise.

"If I had money, I would have never done it!" exclaims Linda Mahoney, founder of Dubai-based real estate company Better Homes.[34] In 1986, pressured by life circumstances, she spotted a gap in the market—a lack of professional real estate agents operating in Dubai.

Since its humble beginnings in a desk in the corner of Mahoney's dining room, Better Homes has since grown to a full-service real estate firm employing nearly five hundred people. Just like Hadi, a hunger of need made Linda do what she would not have done otherwise.

In the corporate world, typical risk mitigation practices act as a roadblock to pursuing the ambition that stems from a hunger in your gut. Practically speaking, risk is the avoidance of losing something. This stands juxtaposed to ambition, which focuses on achieving. The concern is that potential losses almost always seem larger than the potential gain. Because of the desire to avoid anything that smacks of loss, CEOs hesitate to place big bets on new initiatives, instead choosing to focus more on managing the consequences rather than pursing ambitious plans. Sure things are never the big ones.

Ambition is riddled with risk. Rather than trying to manage the risk, be courageous in your pursuit of bold ambition. Don't let others' prudence taper what you can accomplish.

Sheikh Mohammed says, "Life is full of challenges. Risk will not disrupt our plans. If we do not accept risk, we will not accomplish. We must embrace positivity, determination, and the will to achieve."[35]

AMBITION FOR TOMORROW

As Sheikh Rashid began passing the baton in the 1980s, his sons decided to propel Dubai to an entirely different sphere. Despite Dubai's formidable achievements, Sheikh Rashid's sons had their own ambitious plans for Dubai, and for the future.

The central focus of the brothers' plans was to continue the strategic plan of "Hub Dubai" but on a more global level. Though Dubai had grown by leaps and bounds, people were still asking, "Where is Dubai?" Globally speaking, the city was still relatively unknown.

To be a real global hub, Dubai had to become more than a mere stopping point on the modern-day Silk Road, the trade route between Asia and the West. Dubai had to become a destination—a place that everyone knows about and wants to come to. This would require two things, which would build on the fundamentals of the original free-trade play from 1901: first, substantiating the ability to conduct tax-free business and to provide an alternative to requiring a local partner in order to do business (a rare exception in the Middle East for a foreigner). Second, it also required that Dubai become an attractive tourist destination.

"One day a man mistakenly came into my office," shares Sultan Bin Sulayem about his first job as a customs inspector in the late 1970s. "We started chatting and he suggested that Dubai could serve as a trading post for tea if it created a tax-free zone at the port." The idea of building a free zone captured Bin Sulayem's curiosity.

So the following summer vacation he bought an around-the-world plane ticket and set out studying the globe's most preeminent free-trade zones—Hong Kong, South Korea, Singapore, Taiwan, Honolulu, Dallas, and New York. Convinced this was what Jebel Ali needed, he personally took a proposal to Sheikh Mohammed, who had already been quietly studying the idea. Sheikh Mohammed told the thirty-year-old Bin Sulayem, "So if you really believe in it, you go run it."[36]

These free zones permitted foreign companies to establish themselves and operate tax free, while at the same time repatriating funds. Bringing this concept to Dubai legitimized a century-old practice. However, one barrier remained: federal legislation stood in opposition to it. Created in 1984, the UAE's federal "Commercial Companies Law" required all companies to have majority UAE national ownership (at least 51 percent), but the free zones would provide an exception, enabling foreigners to enjoy complete ownership.

The first step to work around this piece of legislation was launching the Jebel Ali Free Zone (commonly referred to as JAFZA), which opened in 1985 next to Jebel Ali Port. The thinking was that foreign companies would have easy access to unloading facilities. JAFZA was also distant from the city center, allowing physical autonomy. Initially, JAFZA wasn't the economic success story that it is today. Only nineteen companies signed up in its first year. People questioned the idea and ambition of Dubai, asking, "Who will ever put their business in JAFZA?" And, again, those proved to be people's famous last words. Today more than six thousand companies are based in JAFZA, including more than 150 of the Fortune Global 500 companies.

The establishment of this deregulated zone encouraged significant expatriate investment. Regional politics also precipitated the flow of merchants to JAFZA. A significant number of businessmen affected by the Iran-Iraq War, and Iraq's invasion of Kuwait, seized the opportunity to establish them-selves in Dubai, where they could now own 100 percent of their company, without the requirement of a local partner.

Yet despite the success of Jebel Ali, Sheikh Rashid's sons had an even grander vision: they wanted to expand the idea behind JAFZA and create free zones for every sector.

The ambition to transition beyond hard-goods trade *deepened* Dubai's original strategy. In 2000, Dubai Internet City and Media City—the cornerstone of TECOM—successfully lured the world's top technology and media companies to build regional headquarters in Dubai.[37] Today Media City, where my office is located, and Internet City are home to thousands of companies that have chosen to make Dubai their headquarters, or at least regional HQ, given its easy access and friendly business environment.

Despite the flow of companies into Dubai, a persistent area of concern was the preexisiting legal framework, specifically enforceability of judicial judgments and overall governance structure. In 2004, the city established the Dubai International Financial Centre (DIFC), which is a federal financial free zone providing financial institutions with the platform to reach into and out of the emerging markets. Dubai seized the opportunity to span the time zones not covered by New York, London, and Hong Kong and to act as a crucial node in global finance. It completed the missing quarter in the twenty-four-hour, seven-days-a-week global financial system.

DIFC is different than the other free zones. It is an independent jurisdiction under the UAE Constitution, with its own civil and commercial laws distinct from those of the wider UAE. DIFC laws and regulations are written in English and default to English law in the event of an ambiguity. The

DIFC also has its own courts, with judges taken from leading common-law jurisdictions including England, Singapore, and Hong Kong. Given its legal structure, DIFC gives Dubai even greater credibility as a place to do business.

Originally, the jurisdiction of the DIFC Courts was limited to the geographical area within the DIFC. Responding to its strategy of creating an environment in which others can succeed, in October 2011, Dubai expanded the role of DIFC Courts, allowing it to hear both local and international cases. Its role would be to resolve commercial disputes with the consent of all parties. In essence, a product could be made in Beijing by an Indian company registered in the Cayman Islands, sold through a website in the UK, and shipped to the Gulf by a US distributor, but a consumer or retailer could insist the DIFC Courts be installed as the legal jurisdiction. Should lawyers be called in, both parties would be facing a showdown in Dubai.[38]

JAFZA, Internet City, Media City, DIFC, and Dubai's other economic zones propelled Dubai into "global powerhouse" status. "Where is Dubai?" was no longer a question. People came to Dubai and stayed. In the 1990s, Dubai held the top position worldwide for both population and employment growth, at 5.8 percent and 8.3 percent per year, respectively. This growth came from clearly holding to the same strategy of creating a place where others can succeed—in other words, a hub that was a favorable place for business.

This ambition for tomorrow also included Dubai's tourism industry—or lack thereof. Dubai needed people to visit, a place for them to stay when they did, and something for them to do. Blessed as it is with year-round sun, sand, and sea, it made sense to make the city a beach destination. To balance out its scorching temperatures, Dubai added a fourth, air-conditioned "S"—shopping.

In 1996 Dubai launched the Dubai Shopping Festival, which offered deep discounts at stores all throughout Dubai, including the malls. It was the first of its kind in the region, attracting a more-than-respectable 1.6 million visitors its first year. Again, Dubai's huge ambition became reality. Today, Dubai's malls draw an astounding 150 million visitors per year.[39]

The developments in the 1990s and 2000s were pure ambition. None of these accomplishments would have happened without it. Sheikh Rashid's sons didn't have to undertake any of these efforts; they could have left well enough alone and rested on the shoulders of their father's success. But real leaders can't; their hunger of habit is too great to ignore. Yesterday's ambition is never sufficient for tomorrow. To lead Dubai style, you need the type of ambition that makes others say, "Impossible!"

In a question-and-answer session during a government summit in 2013, Sheikh Mohammed told the story of how a journalist approached him with a question. "'How much of your vision have you achieved so far, in percentage?' she asked. I am always straightforward, so I gave it some thought and told her: I'm very ambitious, and so are my people and my president. So my answer to her was: 10 percent."

Two years later, the journalist approached Sheikh Mohammed again, but this time it was after the inauguration of the Burj Khalifa (the tallest building in the world), the launch of the Dubai Metro, and the Meydan Racecourse, which accommodates sixty thousand spectators and is home to the Dubai World Cup horse race. The journalist asked, "And now, after completing these mega-projects, how much of your vision have you achieved?"

Said Sheikh Mohammed: "I looked at her and thought about it carefully and answered: 7 percent. She was shocked and protested, because two years back I answered 10 percent. After all these projects, did the percentage decline? I said yes, because when one has a vision, and he is eager to achieve it, one sees, practices, and learns from his mistakes. Therefore, his vision expands and becomes broader over time. This is why, today, I have seen another way that is different to the path I took two years ago."

"Now let's assume that we did achieve everything; what are we to do then?!" the Sheikh asked. "Should we cross our arms and do nothing? Achieving goals is an inspiration and a duty. It is a lifetime mission. There is no finish line when it comes to progress, innovation, and excellence. There's no limit; the sky is the limit."[40]

Mohammed Alabbar, CEO of Emaar, the leading property developer in Dubai, knows all about this hunger. Before supervising the construction of the Burj Khalifa, Alabbar grew up in a home made of date palm fronds and silts from the salt marshes located near the creek, with his mother, father, and twelve siblings. Like many Dubaians at the time, he had no electricity or running water. People depended on candles and kerosene lanterns, locally know as *Fanar*, for lighting their homes. For "air-conditioning," to protect against the brutal summer heat, most homes had a *Bajeel* (wind tower) to ventilate the air and cool the home through the evaporation of floor water under the tower.

Alabbar remembers, "Life was very, very simple, such a basic living. That basic living motivates one to do so much more."[41] This humble upbringing infused him with a driving hunger of habit, a hunger that will likely—to the city's bene-fit—never be abated.

When you have a hunger of habit, you're hungry even when, physically, you're not—that is, when there's no need. This sort of ambition is the habit in leading Dubai style, not the exception. Even when the city was just surviving, its leaders were also succeeding. You've got to be this hungry to achieve grand results.

In Dubai audacity of vision is accepted as an everyday practice!

Dubai's ambitions have always surpassed what others thought possible. Others' doubts never deterred leaders' plans, nor should they yours. A lot of people dream about what could be possible, *if only*. Others may prefer a prudent future without risk, which is fine, if you want to accomplish mediocre things. But if you want big, choose big! Your level of ambition is your choice and will be the guidepost for what you're able to ac-complish.

FIVE

Follow the Leader

——Leadership Habit——
ACT DECISIVELY
AND GIVE DIRECTION

"Kohema . . . two steps to the right!" belted out Officer Cadet (Mohammed bin) Rashid to his fellow officer cadets, who stood in parade formation at Mons Officer Cadet School in Aldershot, England.

It was the austere late 1960s, and everyone at the school (which later became part of Sandhurst) was on edge. Minister of Defense Denis Healey was scheduled to visit that day, and if Healey didn't give the school an operating budget, it would have to shutter its doors.

The facility was at its finest: the buildings had received a fresh coat of paint, the grounds were manicured, and the officer cadets had drilled to peak performance. The students and staff were determined to put on a sterling performance to show why the venerable school should be exempt from the cuts.

But when the commandant, Brigadier Philip Heidenstram, appeared, he was annoyed to find Sheikh Mohammed out of line with the rest of the cadets. Sheikh Mohammed was the Senior Under Officer (SUO), the highest rank possible for a cadet. During the final stages of the six months at Mons, it was traditional to appoint two officer cadets as Junior Under Officers and one as Senior Under Officer, the highest rank that can be held by a cadet. These three officers would take on permanent responsibilities for organizing the company and assume partial leadership over it. So why was Officer Cadet Rashid blowing it on this one day when perfection was required?

Brigadier Heidenstram immediately informed Sergeant-Major Benney, who was in charge of the troops, of his displeasure, which was a subtle but direct order to rectify this misalignment and have the cadets in perfect formation.

"Officer Cadet Rashid!" Benney bellowed. "Take two steps left!"

Instinctively knowing the desired outcome, Officer Cadet Rashid ordered his cadet officers to take two steps to the right. The forty or so cadets quickly adjusted their positions: problem solved, the troops were aligned. The question is: Was this an act of disobedience or a display of leadership genius?

I have to believe it's the latter, that this legendary story shows decisive, action-oriented leadership. Sheikh Mohammed didn't spend time analyzing the order; he knew exactly what Brigadier Heidenstram wanted—alignment, a perfect display for the minister of defense—and had the courage to act rather than to just follow orders.

You may be concerned that there's a risk in not following an exact order, and there is. This was certainly the case in a military setting where there was a clear chain of command: the assumption was that you were to take the order literally. Yet Sheikh Mohammed took the proverbial "hill"—he accomplished the shared sense of the goal without needing a detailed order describing who had to do what. What did the brigadier want? Alignment. Actually, he wanted something even greater—a perfect display for the minister of defense. And that is what he received. As I'll show in the coming pages, it sometimes pays to act decisively, even if it goes against "official" orders.

Strong, outcome-based leadership is prevalent through the "story" of Dubai and is something we can all learn from. The point being, leaders lead!

ACT DECISIVELY

When I reflect on this story and the leadership lineage of Dubai, a foolproof approach to leading becomes clear—autocratic leadership. Not a dictatorship! And also not a totalitarian state, where a leader holds total authority and seeks to control all aspects of life. No, I'm talking about strong, fair autocratic leadership—concentrated decision making, where decisions aren't subject to external restraint. Leaders who act and don't wait on consensus. (I'll go into the perils of "consensus leadership" a bit later.)

In Sheikh Mohammed's case, Sergeant-Major Benney effectively told him to get aligned. The Sheikh then decided on a course of action and communicated it to those in his sphere of influence. He had the courage and boldness to act. This habit says leaders decide and then direct others, giving a clear outcome to achieve—that is, "Take the hill."

This is the essence of autocratic leadership: when the leader speaks, the people act! In an autocratic environment, senseless and endless discussion is unnecessary, even unwelcomed. You make the decision about what to do and direct your people to do it. When I think of an autocratic leader, I think of someone who isn't afraid to take the power of authority, even without relying on his or her positional authority.

I know the mention of an autocrat tends to conjure up images of an offensively self-assured leader, some jerk who has a bossy way of ordering others around. Michael Eisner, former CEO of The Walt Disney Company, might be an example who comes to mind. While he accomplished unprecedented success for himself and for the company, he was infamous for his insensitive leadership style. Eisner didn't listen to anyone; he had no ear for others' opinions. He wasn't patient, and he simply didn't think anyone in the company was worthy enough of his time or interest. He micromanaged Disney and put his stamp on everything that the company did.

But when used in its purity, autocracy can be a very potent and successful form of leadership. It doesn't require your being a bossy jerk, a dictator who casts out others. It merely reclaims the work of leaders: to lead. A "good" autocrat is a leader who isn't afraid to make decisions, who is clear about what outcome he wants, and who can lead his troops to success. And one who cares for his people. Caring for people is what separates the benevolent autocrats from the negative type. Let's again be clear: the style of autocratic leadership we're speaking of here isn't the aggravating and domineering type.

I certainly wouldn't want to work for that "type" of autocrat: the offensive ones who lord their unlimited and unwarranted power over people's heads. There's a name for these types of "bossy characters" who order everyone around:

LINOs (Leaders in Name Only). LINOs have the position and the title, yet don't act as leaders. Their behavior isn't aligned with the spirit of this habit. It is an abuse of the position.

TAKE RESPONSIBILITY

Over the years, I've frequently seen autocratic leadership—*the results-oriented leadership style*—used as a "negative" example in textbooks and business school courses. I had to wonder: *Why?*

One reason may be that we've been programmed to think that "collective" leadership (collaboration, consensus, democratic, or whatever you want to call it) is better than "centralized" leadership (autocratic, directive). A walk through any bookstore or a scan of contemporary thoughts on leadership highlights the obsession with the consensus-style leader, which in the day-to-day activities gets confused with an all-inclusive-style leader. "Inclusive" leaders involve everyone, believing that each person has a voice and that the group should go with the consensus. That's not leadership; it's diplomacy.

Leaders should definitely listen, and they should involve others, but at the end of the day the leader is a leader to act. (Of course, leaders should always act in the best interest of the company and its people.) As a leader you are the shepherd of your team, company, or in the case of Dubai, a city. You are responsible! In the metaphorical sense, could you imagine the shepherd asking his sheep where to move to next? He would get as many different opinions as there are sheep in the herd. Consensus would be a time-draining trap. Instead, the shepherd moves the herd forward. He leads them to a better tomorrow, one where they will succeed.

I am not equating employees or citizens to sheep, but the illustration does highlight a drawback of consensus—too many opinions and too much time.

A common concern is that autocratic leadership lacks good governance and can be a breeding ground for corruption. Regrettably, examples of corrupt leaders consolidating power to their advantage abound, and that is typically what we hear when we listen to stories about strong, centralized leadership. While journalists love to make examples of these "bad apples," they fail to tell the other side of the story—the positive results that this style achieves. Being directive isn't an excuse for not listening or being a jerk. And it's not a reason to cast out others. It merely reclaims the work of leaders—to lead: make decisions, give direction, and empower people to act.

Corporate corridors are full of positive examples of decisive, action-oriented leaders. A short list of highly respected centralized, autocratic leaders includes the likes of Ralph Lauren, John Chambers, Henry Ford, Walt Disney, the Carnegies, the Rockefellers, the Vanderbilts, and nearly every leader whose actions led to great results. Apple CEO Steve Jobs was a poster boy for autocratic leadership. He wasn't the best delegator when it came to making directional decisions, but he delegated the delivery of the vision to his team of experts, and, never relenting, he got what he wanted.

The great advantage of strong, decisive leadership is speed and clarity—something that's almost always lacking in board-structured leadership. A board acts on behalf of, and is subordinate to, the business' owners, which usually chooses the members of the board, oftentimes getting trapped between competing interests. Leading Dubai style is the opposite: it is outcome focused, courageous, and decisive. Leaders make decisions with speed and authority, never getting bogged down by what the "board thinks is best."

Dubai's aviation industry has in large part been successful as a result of not having boards. The airport, Emirates Airline, DNATA, and Dubai Duty Free have all achieved unparalleled feats due to their autocratic leadership structure, with Sheikh Ahmed bin Saeed at the helm. They are among the fastest growing, biggest, and best in the world—all with very short histories.

Recalled Maurice Flanagan, "Sheikh Mohammed gave his greatest gift, [which] was Sheikh Ahmed. . . He is a brilliant chairman, he really is."[42] Sheikh Ahmed knows everything that's going on in his companies. In addition to his elephantine memory, which is like a steel trap, and his formidable intellect, he is respected for being decisive. Each of his direct reports—who are in their own right the top global industry leaders—speak of the fact that they can take any issue needing his attention to him and an outcome will be decided.

Paul Griffiths, CEO of Dubai Airports, continually credits Sheikh Ahmed's leadership style as a contributor to the airport and Dubai's success. "Anytime I go to him, he decides. There is no need for a committee," Griffiths shares. No committees, rarely a request for an additional study—a decision is made and they move forward. He's even commented that given the democratic decision-making process in the UK, there's no way that Heathrow could move with the speed that Dubai's airports can. Implying, what takes years to build here, could take lifetimes there.

While autocracy practices centralized decision making, it is collaborative in nature. To be a good autocrat, you need to be inclusive, informed, and considerate. Every person's opinion matters. However, that doesn't mean you hand the reins to your people. Instead you *seek their opinion*—the core practice in the majlis—*before* you act decisively. A good autocrat doesn't strive to control every aspect of life, nor does he bow to the whims of the people: his job is to walk that line with skill and care.

Toward the other end of the spectrum, democracy encourages every opinion to be involved in actually making the decision. This system gives the power to the masses, encourages the rule of the people, and fosters bureaucracy, which ends up leading to slower action. Relying on group projects and the currently popular "matrix" style of management tends to fail because group members are constrained by the pace of one another.

In Dubai the advantages of the autocratic style when compared with the democratic process are clear. If Dubai employed the "rule of the people" model we wouldn't have an enlarged creek, nor would we have Al Maktoum Bridge, Jebel Ali, or the Mall of the Emirates. Remember: The "people" went to Sheikh Mohammed beseeching him to convince his father to cease with the idea of Port Jebel Ali. The "people" from the community questioned Majid Al Futtaim's sanity in building the Mall of the Emirates. If left to their own devices at the ballot box, "the people" surely wouldn't have voted for the expansion of the city.

Frankly, there's a reason for all this. Most people aren't leaders, so they decide with a follower mentality rather than a leader's focus. But what this means is that people expect, and even desire, leadership. They wish for a leader who leads!

LEAD IN YOUR SPHERE OF INFLUENCE

Keep in mind that autocratic leadership doesn't mean there's just one leader. Not every decision needs to or should be made by the CEO. The idea of this chapter is to emphasize that leaders—not just the CEO or senior management, but all leaders—make decisions. They're decisive! They decide in line with what is at their level of responsibility, in other words in the sphere of influence they have earned. Never should you push upward a decision that can be made at your level, nor should you step down and make decisions that others should be making.

I'm hesitant to use this example, as it's possible it will give the wrong idea, but the Dubai leadership style operates like a non-militaristic army that doesn't rely on the "sword" we mentioned earlier for control. At the delivery level Dubai has the hierarchical structure that the military enjoys. Malcolm Wall Morris, former CEO of the Dubai Multi Commodities Center (DMCC), a government entity that enhances commodity trade flows and is Dubai's largest free zone, describes it like this: "Dubai operates like an army. At the head is the field marshal, His Highness [or in the private sector, the owner], who gives the mission that is to be carried out, which is not questioned and debated. Below are the generals and colonels—the director generals and CEOs who have to figure out how to do it. They turn the mission into a course of action. As the directions pass down the food chain, they become more specific while still allowing for flexibility in execution."[43] The focus is always on the outcome and delegating responsibility to deliver. The expectation is for leaders to lead at each level.

Osman Sultan, CEO of du Telecom, sums the situation up perfectly by saying, "You have to be stubborn on a vision and flexible on the execution." A good autocrat leads, but also gives his or her lieutenants the freedom to act as long as it's in line with the desired outcomes. Throughout Dubai's history, its leaders have decided *what* is to be accomplished, not *how* to do it.

As Wall Morris mentioned, at the top level the directives are broad. For example, the Sheikh might say to Paul Griffiths, the CEO of the airport, "Don't do anything to constrain the global aviation industry."[44] Then Griffiths would turn that mission into an operational order—for example, "Let's expand the capacity of the airports to support growth until 2050." His team would then turn the order into specific actions giving direction to their teams on how to drive the growth of the airport. What makes this model so effective is that the chain of command isn't questioned. It demands and gives full loyalty, full leadership.

The latitude given to the leaders here in the form of missions is enormous, almost carte blanche. You can effectively do what you want in your sphere of authority, at your level. But it comes with a clear expectation to deliver in line with Dubai's strategy at the level of your responsibility. The more latitude a leader has, the more self-discipline he needs to employ. It is perfectly clear that results are required—this is unwavering.

The success of this style in large part comes down to the type of directions the leader gives. They should be commensurate with the level of leadership. The CEO gives direction for the company, and a team leader for the team. Not the inverse. Can you imagine a Ruler like Sheikh Mohammed giving direction at the team level? I can't either. Leaders who step completely out of their level—whether upward or downward—to give direction are abusing the possibility of this style.

PERSUADE TO PERFORM

You may have been taught that you should make decisions in a way that allows everybody to agree with those decisions in order to get their buy-in. The idea is that the success rate will be higher with the backing of all the people, even if the decision isn't the best one. But why would you settle for a second-best decision? The leadership habit discussed in this chapter is about giving direction.

The idea that people will support the outcome because they had input is a flawed understanding. Consensus decision making isn't the only way to gain support. Rather, you need to have the vision and charisma to persuade your team to support what they sometimes don't understand, what they may not want to or even know they need to do. In his majlis, Sheikh Rashid would often talk men into supporting his ideas, men who just hours earlier thought what he proposed was improbable. He persuaded his people to do what was best for Dubai, even when they couldn't see or comprehend it. Always, the power of persuasion beats the theoretical idea of allowing everybody to decide in order to get their "buy-in."

Had it been left to the employees, Dubai would not have created an e-government. One friend to another asked, "Why do we need e-government?" as they walked out of the 1999 meeting where Sheikh Mohammed gathered all the government employees to announce the creation of e-government in Dubai. "You're right, we are doing great! Why this change?" This sentiment permeated the conversation as they waited for their cars from the valet. Yet Sheikh Mohammed didn't let their apprehension dissuade him; instead he persuaded them, and Dubai became the first country in the Arab world to adopt e-government.

We can see the power of this sort of persuasion through-out Dubai's history. Which citizens in 1833 were thinking about a third form of government? Yet they followed Sheikh Maktoum bin Butti through the desert, and generations are benefiting from this decision. This is leading Dubai style—"pure" autocratic decision making that keeps others' benefit in mind.

To use a more recent example, I can't imagine the use of democracy in deciding to build the Palm Jumeirah, the "Eighth Wonder of the World" and one of Dubai's biggest tourist attractions, which now houses four thousand luxury villas and apartments, along with more than thirty hotels. Per-haps "the people" would have discussed it, but "decided"? No! They'd still be debating the logic of building a man-made palm-shaped island in the middle of the Arabian Sea, and the need to increase Dubai's shoreline by more than five hundred kilometers, when there were already seventy existing kilome-ters. It takes guts to make tough decisions!

Real leaders lead. They make decisions. They take action. Don't fall into the democratic trap of thinking that everyone decides together. You do have a duty to listen to others, but then you must act decisively.

Have no fear: such a fair, empowering autocratic lead-ership model has the potential to achieve spectacular results, without harming others in the process. Always remember that you are expected to decide and lead in accordance with your level of accountability.

SIX

Focus

Intrigued by the idea that leaders pick hobbies reflecting their leadership habits, I recently asked an award-winning equestrian endurance racer, who is also a leading Emirati businessman, "What have you learned about leading from your hobby?"

He paused. "That's a good question you ask. . . . It would be three points: your horse wants to run, take care of your horse first, and where you look, your horse will go."

An equestrian endurance race is the equivalent of a marathon, except instead of running, you ride. It is a grueling race extending up to 160-kilometers over natural terrain—you could say a cross-county "trail"—that lasts upward of ten hours, depending on how good of a rider you are. Sometimes it starts before dawn and ends after sunset. The races take place in every conceivable climate and terrain—from hot, forbidding races in wind-blown deserts to freezing-cold races in forests and mountains.

All along the course, periodic veterinary checks are required to make sure the horse is still in good health and fit enough to continue. The mandatory maximum allowable heart rate is typically sixty beats per minute. This acts like a throttle on how hard the rider can push his horse. If the horse's heart rate exceeds the maximum allowable rate, the rider has to wait for the horse's heart rate to slow down. All the while, the rider's time keeps on ticking.

Because of the nature of this sport, every caution is taken to ensure the safety and health of the horses. Both the rider and horse must finish in good condition no matter how rough the ride.

As this champion rider points out, making sure the horse is running hard, even at his peak, but not breaking him, is every rider's foremost concern. "You need to drive the horse to utilize its energy but not drive it so fast that you deplete its energy," he shared. After all, horses love to run and they want to run hard. But it is the jockey's role to know just how hard the horse can run without breaking. Therefore, the rider must have a great knowledge of pace, knowing when to slow down or speed up during the ride, as well as a great knowledge of his horse's condition and signs of tiring. It's the same for a leader: your people want to work hard! You have to know exactly how hard you can push your employees without their breaking, and then make sure they work at their peak. Too hard and they'll break. Not enough and they'll get soft and lose their motivation.

In a marathon, there are water stations every five kilometers so the runner can grab a drink to combat dehydration. Similarly, there are water stops along the trail in an endurance race. Interestingly, the rider gives the water first to the horse to cool him down. The welfare of the horse is paramount. Another great leadership point—take care of your people first.

Yet the leadership point that resonated most with me was the last one: "Where you look, your horse will go." Horses sense even the slightest movement, so an expert jockey must maintain complete focus for hours on end. "You can't be distracted," says this champion. "You have to concentrate." In other words, no letting go of the reins.

Hours into these physically challenging races, it is tempting for even the most seasoned jockey to be distracted by what is happening around him. "You can't," my contact emphasized. Distractions along the race can prevent you from crossing the finish line first. If you want to win, you have to stay 100 percent focused on your destination. There's no time to enjoy the scenery if you want to win. The work of the leader is to stay focused on the course, even if he or she has been "on the back of the horse" for an interminably long time.

KEEP YOUR EYE ON THE TARGET

In business, as in a horse race, where you look, so will your employees. When their focus shifts, execution problems emerge. Like the rider who shifts his focus for a fraction of a second and cedes his victory as a result, when you get distracted, you put you and your team's goals at risk.

In a typical horse race, the horse wears blinkers, also known as blinders, to prevent it from seeing to the rear and in some cases to the side. But the blinkers aren't enough to keep the horse on course. The horse actually takes its cues from the jockey. Where the jockey looks, he leans—even if it's ever so slightly—causing the horse to veer off course. What you talk about will determine where your employees look. Keep your eye on the target.

Imagine the focus that was required in the 1960s to turn a primitive trading village into a global city full of skyscrapers. Many of the residents had never experienced, even on holiday, the structures Sheikh Rashid was building. So at every turn, he reminded people of his exact focus. One day while visiting one of the small shops in town, he picked up and peered into a child's View-Master, marveling at the 3-D images of the Statue of Liberty and the Empire State Building. Then he turned to the store's owner and said, "One day, you will see tall buildings here." In his mind, he saw a Dubai like New York City. Leading is being obsessed with a precise idea that is bigger than your individual ability to deliver, so you inspire others to carry through with it.

Not everyone understood or was supportive of Sheikh Rashid's ideas. Preposterous! is what most people called the Dubai World Trade Centre, which became the tallest building in the Middle East at the time. Many people laughed at what was happening, not seeing the need for such buildings. Over the decades, you could substitute the Dubai World Trade Centre with nearly any other major project and still hear the same refrain: "It's crazy!" The people were looking at today, not tomorrow.

It is easy to stay focused on your strategy when everyone thinks it's a good idea. But people will question the strategy; they won't always be supportive and won't see the future the way you do. Still, you must stay focused! In Sheikh Rashid's story, we see what a true leader has to do—focus everyone else on the strategy even when they don't want to. Leading is never easy!

As we'll discuss in the next section, clearly communicating what you expect from your team is one of the most important things you, as a leader, can do to maintain focus.

COMMUNICATE CLEARLY

Too many leaders I see suffer from what I call the "I Can Complete My Thought Later" disease. While this disease doesn't have a medical or scientific basis, I discovered it over years of close leader observation, and it goes something like this: As a leader, you have an idea, a sketch in your mind of what you want. You give a vague description to your team, who then heads off to work on it. When what they bring back is far from what you had in mind, only then do you give more detail. All along you had the ability to give a more precise picture, but because you were really busy, or assumed that others had the same idea in their minds, you didn't. Subconsciously, you knew that you could complete your thought later. Sound familiar?

When you choose not to convey a crystal-clear idea, you cost your team time and effort, forcing them to redo work—doing something twice or three times, when it could have been done right the first time. So be sure to ask yourself next time you have to communicate a vision: Do you know what you want? Does your team?

To illustrate the effects of the I Can Complete My Thought Later disease, when I'm working with a group of executives, I ask them to draw a house. After a minute or so, I look at their pictures and start asking, "Where is the second floor? Where is the fence? The chimney?" (Or whatever is missing from what I originally had in my mind.) Inevitably, the response is, "But you didn't ask for those elements; you just asked for a house!" This exercise is a perfect example of the disease's negative impact on performance—that is, causing people to repeat work they could have done correctly the first time. As a leader you need to know exactly what you want and focus on this when you convey directions to your team. Otherwise, everyone around you will get distracted, just as the horse does when the jockey glances off to the side.

The autocratic—or centralized decision-making—approach lends itself to having "one voice," and a corresponding clarity of direction. Sheikh Mohammed always makes sure that what he wants is very clear. Rarely do people have to repeat work, as in the previous example. He calls everyone in when he wants to pass on a message—maybe through a special lunch or a gathering in his majlis. Since taking over as Ruler, he's been fond of hosting government summits that bring all the employees together in one place. After handing down his clearly stated order, he leaves you to get after it, to execute the plan. This style frees his ranks from the effects of the I Can Complete My Thought Later disease.

In 1983 Mohi-Din Binhendi, director general of Dubai Aviation, hired Colm McLoughlin, general manager of Shannon (Ireland) Duty Free, to make Dubai Airport's Duty Free shopping area the best in the world.

"Make it the best!" were Colm McLoughlin's original marching orders. At the time the airport had only a handful of random shops. Really, it was a fledging operation. But the mandate (focus) coming from Sheikh Mohammed was clear: make it the best. Sheikh Mohammed knew what he wanted, and so did the new general manager.

Two years later in 1985, Dubai Duty Free (DDF) was named the "Airport Duty Free Operator of the Year" by *Frontier* magazine, the longest-serving magazine covering the travel retail industry. This was the first of 475 awards DDF would earn over the next thirty years. A few years later, after DDF retained its position as being the best, Sheikh Mohammed, perhaps in jest, upped the ante. "Now make it the biggest," came the charge.

And it is! DDF accounts for 5.19 percent of global airport duty free business and almost 3 percent of the wider duty free and global travel retail business. According to an analysis by independent researcher Generation Research,[45] DDF is the world's largest single airport retail operation, with $1.8 billion in sales in 2013.[46] As Sheikh Mohammed often says, "We should always be number one because nobody remembers number two."

In 2007, *60 Minutes* (CBS's long-running newsmagazine program) posed the following questions to Sheikh Mohammed: "What are you trying to do here? What do you want this place to be?"

"I want it to be number one," said the Sheikh, calmly. "Not in the region, but in the world."

Explaining what he meant by "number one in the world," he said, "In everything—higher education, health, and housing. Just making my people (have) the highest way of living."

"And why do you want everything to be the biggest, the tallest?" reporter Steve Kroft asked.

His Highness challenged, "Why not?"[47]

EVOKE HONOR

The Sheikh's interview reminds us of one of the recurring ways to maintain focus in Dubai: by public declaration, where the *mudir* (boss) makes a visible statement for everyone to hear about what will be accomplished. Because these expectations are made in a public forum, it invokes a sense of honorable duty to deliver.

I guess you could say, "Announce it and they will do it."

A good example of "pure" public declaration, Dubai style, is Sheikh Mohammed's announcement of the Mall of the World project in July 2014. Overlooking a model of the temperature-controlled city—the first of its kind in the world—Sheikh Mohammed shared that the Mall of the World would welcome 180 million visitors per year. (The planet's largest mall as of this writing, Dubai Mall, attracts some eighty million visitors per year.) In turn, the forty-eight-million square-foot complex, which will include a domed theme park, hotels, apartments, and stores, will become the world's largest shopping mall/entertainment complex.

"Our ambitions are higher than having seasonal tourism," said Sheikh Mohammed. "Tourism is a key driver of our economy, and we aim to make the UAE an attractive destination all year long. This is why we will start working on providing pleasant temperature-controlled environments during the summer months. We are confident of our economy's strength, optimistic about our country's future, and we continue to broaden our vision."[48]

While this announcement was exciting, it was clear that he was expecting Dubai Holding, the developer behind the project, to deliver. Not only would Dubai Holding be representing their own performance character—the persistence, self-discipline, and grit needed to get things done and achieve excellence in performance—they were also reflecting His Highness's and all of Dubai's credibility.

This approach to motivation is based on using the regional concept of honor and shame. An oversimplified way of viewing this type of honor is to think of it as the reflection of one's reputation and the respect it brings as it places one in society's eyes. This powerful concept affects both one's social standing and self-evaluation, and is a backbone quality across the Middle East and Asia. Leveraging this specific code has proven to be a powerful motivator of performance in Dubai.

Ahmed bin Butti, former director general of Dubai Customs, sums honor and shame up as: "When you do good things, you help your family. And when you do wrong, you hurt your family."[49]

Shame is to be avoided at all costs in Dubai. Shame arises when one's defects are exposed to others; in the case of a public declaration, that defect would be a lack of delivery on a project. An example of this is the overzealous Nakheel Tower, promised in the mid-2000s by Dubai developer Nakheel to rise one kilometer above an inner-city harbor. Due to the Financial Crisis of 2008, Nakheel never broke ground on the project. This type of shame may not only cost you your job: its repercussions affect all who are connected. As we will see in the "Circle of Loyalty" chapter, just as honor is communal, shame smears the group.

If I were to translate the practice of "positive" public declaration into corporate leadership, it is simply the practice of making everyone's performance objectives and progress public. The honor method of motivation says that because the objectives are shared with others, and others are dependent on you, you will deliver because it is now the honorable action.

Another good example of a showstopping public declaration was Sheikh Rashid's announcements in the 1940s, while he was Crown Prince, about the government's heavy investments in education and health care, beginning with Al Maktoum Hospital, which would be the first modern medical facility on the Trucial Coast.[50] The local newspaper reported, "The activity was non-stop. For every Rs. 50,000 from custom dues he [Sheikh Rashid] would start another project costing six million."[51] By announcing these projects openly, he was evoking the future honor of those who were entrusted to deliver on them.

The practice of public declaration has continued largely unchanged over the decades, with the only major differences now being how the announcements are relayed and, of course, the magnitude of the new projects. In the 1940s, Sheikh Rashid made his announcement about the new school and hospital in the intimacy of his majlis. Today global media cover the announcements about Dubai's mega-projects. Yet no matter what format the announcement takes, or who's making the announcement, the principle remains the same—now that the public is aware, we're all watching you deliver.

Tim Clark, president of Emirates Airline, used a presentation in October 2013 to the delegates of the Bureau International des Expositions (BIE), to remind everyone that the goal of the airline wasn't to be the biggest in the world, but to "connect travelers from around the world to Dubai and other destinations with just a single stop via our hub" shifting the focus to the real goal. The delegates were visiting the UAE to make their final decision on the host city for EXPO 2020. Clark continued, "The strategic location of Dubai makes it possible for us to serve almost 90 percent of the world's population with nonstop flights. . . . Our location is our key advantage."[52] Because declarations like these clearly tell everyone what the priority is—what the boss wants to see—they evoke honor. (And they evoke respect! One month after Clark's speech, Dubai won the bid to host EXPO 2020.)

It's important to keep in mind that these "honor" announcements never come as a shock to those who are expected to deliver them. The decisions might seem "quick" or "impetuous," but they're always involved and informed. Careful planning precedes every announcement. Leading Dubai style is never about gambling: it is about aggressively taking well-considered risks.

PUT A PLAN IN PLACE

In Dubai what counts is the execution of the vision, and this requires a solid work plan. In other words, a detailed plan with specific deliverables that keep the plan on track. To deliver on a vision, there must be a simplicity and consistency of approach.

"Every ambition has a timetable, and every goal has a time target,"[53] says Sheikh Mohammed. Deadlines aren't an ultimatum, but a normal leadership habit.

Responding to the mission given to Dubai Airports, Paul Griffiths says, "My job is to make sure the airport infrastructure grows to ensure there are no constraints." Over the past fifty years, passenger traffic has increased at an average annual growth rate of 15.5 percent. A 2011 study conducted by global advisory firm Oxford Economics revealed that aviation supports 250,000 jobs—19 percent of Dubai's employment and $22 billion, or 28 percent, of Dubai's GDP. By 2020, those numbers are expected to increase to 22 percent of employment (372,900 jobs) and 32 percent of Dubai's forecasted GDP ($45.4 billion).[54] The only way that Dubai's aviation sector will achieve these numbers is by adhering to strict deadlines, many of which are outlined in the airport's generation-spanning 2050 Plan, "The Airport of the Future."

Vivid insights into the role of strategic planning in Dubai come from Ahmed Hassan Al Shaikh's doctoral work.[55] He shows clearly how Dubai's emphasis on planning and executing the plan directly relates to its unparalleled achievements. For example, beginning in 1996 with Dubai's first formal strategic plan for the development of the city, entitled "Into the Twenty-First Century: A Strategic Plan to Build a Fully Diversified and Prosperous Economy,"[56] Dubai's leaders focused the efforts of government and business leaders toward a better, more prosperous future. As the plan states, "[The] contraction suffered by the economy of Dubai during much of the 1980's has been a sharp reminder of the urgent need for concerted policy measures and other systemic efforts for steering and managing the economy. . . ." This led to the creation of comprehensive, coordinated, and continuous means to attain the city's economic goals, which were the same as always: to sustain the inhabitants' high income level and to further strengthen economic diversification.

Following the successful delivery of the 1996 plan, Dubai published its second formal strategic plan, "New Dubai in a New Economy" in 2003.[57] The plan's focus was on attaining the status and orientation of a developed economy through the strength of the non-oil sectors by 2010. Achieving the results early, in 2007 a new plan was published: "Dubai . . .

Where the Future Begins."[58] Unlike the previous plans, this one was made publically available. Dubai's planning process continues to this day with the latest plan, "Dubai Plan 2021," published in December 2014.[59] This plan describes the future of Dubai through holistic and complementary perspectives, starting with the people and the society who have always been, and always will be, the bedrock of the city. This perspective describes the characteristics that Dubai's people need to have to deliver on the city's aspirations in all areas, and examines the society needed to support and empower these individuals in achieving their goals.[60]

The adherence to delivering on—even exceeding—the plan is what keeps everyone focused. Walking to the escalator outside the Capital Club in DIFC with Andrew Shaw, CEO of Ducab, which supplies power cables and accessories to customers in more than forty countries, he said: "They [a leading consulting firm] have never seen such adherence, as Dubai's, to delivering on a plan. Top businesses in the world do not even execute their strategies with the same fervor." As I looked back over my shoulder through the buildings of the DIFC, I chuckled in agreement, seeing Emirates Towers and the Dubai World Trade Center as physical evidence. Execution is what Dubai is known for.

When you jump on the back of your "horse" (physically or figuratively) at the beginning of the endurance "race," you know what you want to accomplish—to win. Yet you need a solid plan in place in order to do so. Sheikh Mohammed, winner of the 2012 FEI World Endurance Championships in the UK, says, "At the beginning of the race the weather was remarkably unstable, forcing us to cope, in turn, with rain, bitter cold, and wind. In an endurance race, you are constantly adapting your plan according to your horse's capabilities, as well as the terrain and length of the race. . . . The challenge lies in balancing all of these variables, but with God's help I was able to come [in] first in this international race, raising the profile of my company and taking home a gold medal."[61]

Essentially, he said, "Know your target. Have a plan. And more importantly, execute to reach your target."

Where the leader looks, the people will go. It's that simple: you are the GPS. Not only should you be decisive, but you need to keep tunnel vision on the target. Don't get distracted by what's on the right or left; instead keep looking straight ahead. Give clear direction and keep everyone singularly focused. In other words, put the blinkers on!

SEVEN

The Monitor

——Leadership Habit——
MICRO-MONITOR
WITHOUT MICROMANAGING

One morning during his post–Fajr prayers monitoring ses-
sions, Sheikh Rashid noticed progress had stalled on a
particular construction project: the building had halted on the
first floor. As we've seen, he took a hands-on approach to gov-
erning Dubai and was obsessed with checking on the progress
of the development of his city, and not only government projects but also those in the private sector. Given the Sheikh's obsession with progress, this lack of progress was unacceptable,
and something had to be done.

Later that morning, the owner happened to walk into
Sheikh Rashid's majlis, where the heads of the merchant families were gathered. Sheikh Rashid called him to have a seat
beside him.

"How's your family?" Sheikh Rashid asked. A lesser
leader would have put the building owner on the spot, but
Sheikh Rashid was above that mentality. Instead he asked

more and more details about the owner's family, life, and business. After this "idle" chitchat, he casually asked about the status of the building. The owner replied something like, "It is going superbly."

"Really?" Sheikh Rashid responded.

"Yes, it is up to the third floor." What was the man doing lying about his project, to the Ruler nonetheless? It was bad enough to be behind schedule, but to exaggerate the results surely seemed like the kiss of death.

Instead of ripping the owner to shreds, however, Sheikh Rashid replied, "Wow! You must have the best contractor in the universe."

"Well, thank you, Your Highness, but why do you say this?" queried the owner.

"When I was there a few hours ago," the Ruler said, "the building was just on the first floor."

The owner quickly came up with excuses. "Every day, I get reports from the contractor telling me how well the building is progressing—"

"Don't rely on what your contractor or anyone tells you," the Sheikh interrupted, making a clear point to anyone who could hear him, which was everyone. He leaned forward to garner their attention. "Go and see for yourself. Monitor the progress if you want to achieve results." Effectively he said, "Follow my example."

The owner received the message loud and clear, as did the other leaders present. And the legend of the story lives on today.

MICRO-MONITORING

While researching for this book, I was told this story more than a dozen times. When I first heard it from Tariq Lootah, minister of state, I asked, "Do you think Dubai would be what it is today without this type of monitoring?" The immediate reply was "No!" Monitoring is leading Dubai style.

When I first heard this story, I immediately thought of high school hall monitors; that is, "robocops" who try to maintain overall good conduct in the hallways by preventing rowdy behavior and enforcing the school's rules. Unsurprisingly, hall monitors are universally unpopular. Whenever you run into one, you're sure to be questioned, assuming as they do that you're "guilty until proven innocent."

Then I realized that what Sheikh Rashid was doing was different. He wasn't being a "corporate hall monitor." Sheikh Rashid was "micro-monitoring" in the best sense of the word. He knew that for Dubai to succeed, he had to shape high-performance behavior. He accepted this was his responsibility and made it his priority.

"Micro" is, of course, a five-letter-word in management-speak, conjuring up images of dreadful "micro-managing" bosses. These "leaders" observe in order to control—excessively so—the work of subordinates. A micromanager gives too much attention to the minor details, telling his employees what to do and then how to do it, every tiny bit.

Micro-monitoring, on the other hand, isn't a desire to interfere; it's a tactic to make sure people are delivering. Sheikh Rashid's motive wasn't to denigrate the owner for underperformance. It was to prod him forward to deliver according to the plan. Sheikh Rashid never set out to find people's faults. And, neither should you. Like the Sheikh, you should instead be obsessed with seeing everyone succeed.

Micro-monitoring is what leaders do proactively and informally to make sure their employees, teams, and organizations deliver. Obviously you can't know everything that's going on inside of your business, but you must make sure everyone else is obsessed with the details. It is your responsibility to walk the shop floor so you can help people succeed. As we will see later, this is a means of building their capability and behavior.

The confusion of this point is in the difference between micro-monitoring, which is a positive leadership action, and micromanaging, which, as I noted before, is a management curse word. A micromanager frequently requests unnecessary and overly detailed reports as a means of "checking up" on his subordinates.

Think about it—an after-the-fact report merely states what's been done or not done. At this point, there isn't a thing you can do other than state the obvious—you didn't deliver. Wouldn't employees already know this? Of course they would. Still, micro-managers tend to require constant and detailed performance reports focusing excessively on procedural trivia rather than on overall performance, quality, and results, which is what Sheikh Rashid was focused on.

This focus on "low-level" trivia clouds overall goals and objectives, confusing the worker about what's genuinely important, thereby delaying actions. Many micro-managers accept such inefficiencies in hopes of retaining control or at least the appearance of control. By contrast, the micro-monitor gives the control away, keeping his concern on creating an environment in which others must deliver.

Perhaps most importantly, a pattern of micromanagement suggests to employees that a manager doesn't trust their work or judgment. It is a major factor in triggering employee disengagement, often to the point of promoting a dysfunction in which one or more managers, or even management generally, are labeled "control freaks." Disengaged employees invest time but not effort or creativity in the work they're assigned.

There's one other leadership "micro" you need to be aware of—"micro-doing," where leaders take "control" to the extreme and actually do for their employees what the employees could do for themselves. In the midst of frustration, seeing that what should be happening isn't happening in the way he or she wants, a manager becomes a "worker" again and performs the duties assigned to an employee. When a boss performs a worker's job more efficiently than the worker does, the result is merely suboptimal. The organization suffers lost opportunities because the leader would serve the organization better by doing his or her own job.

I've learned that when I initially present the concept of micro-monitoring to my clients, there's an immediate backlash. "But micro-monitoring is wrong!" they exclaim as they confuse it with micromanaging. So, we need to again draw a distinction in terms—micromanaging is telling your team how to do something. Micro-doing is doing the work for them. And micro-monitoring is ensuring that the "what"—the outcome—is being accomplished.

Why did the minister of state so empathetically declare that Dubai wouldn't be what it is today without micro-monitoring? Because micro-monitoring is the "daily" engine that drives Dubai's success.

MONITORING SHOWS YOU CARE

In Dubai, being "micro-monitored" can actually be a source of pride. Gerald Lawless, president and group CEO of Jumeirah Group, which owns some of Dubai's premier hotels, recalled a late-night phone call from Sheikh Mohammed with a smile.

"It was 1:00 a.m. and a voice came on the line. It said, 'Speak to His Highness.' Sheikh Mohammed came on the line. 'How good are the lights in the new ballroom at Jumeirah Beach Hotel?' he asked."

Jumeirah Beach Hotel, the first of Jumeirah's properties, had just opened on Jumeirah Beach Road, on the site of the storied Chicago Beach Hotel. Though way out of town, the Chicago Beach Hotel had helped usher in the tourist industry in Dubai, offering resort-style accommodation and guaranteed sunshine. A government event the next day would be one of the first to take place in the new hotel's ballroom.

Lawless replied to the Sheikh, "We invested significantly to make sure we have the best possible lights."

"Great, I'll meet you there in twenty minutes!" responded Sheikh Mohammed.

A walk-through in the middle of the night: Shouldn't Lawless have been boiling with rage? After all, he was the CEO of Jumeirah Hotels. Lawless quickly put on the suit that he leaves hanging on the back of his bedroom door for such middle of the night "emergency" calls and rushed right over to the hotel, making it in eighteen minutes.

His Highness strolled in at 2:00 a.m., chuckling. "Wasn't it nice of me to let you sleep a few extra minutes? Now show me those lights."

After walking up on the stage, the Sheikh inspected the lights, asking his entourage how they looked. Then he walked back over to Lawless, saying, "We are going to look great tomorrow when CNN is here. Thanks and have a good night."[62]

Micromanaging or micro-monitoring? Did Sheikh Mohammed tell Lawless how to do his job? No! Did he do it for him? Definitely not! He wanted to make sure that Lawless, Jumeirah, and Dubai would look the best they could the next day. He was proactively monitoring to make sure success would come—removing any margin of error.

What struck me most about this story was the way that Lawless smiled when he told it to me. He wasn't upset by it, and he didn't feel personally offended that Sheikh Mohammed was inspecting in so much detail. Actually, he was rather happy about it. You could see it in Lawless' eyes as he retold this story almost two decades later: *The Sheikh cared so much about every detail that he called me in the middle of the night!* The Sheik's actions left an impression on Lawless, and today this story embodies the pride of leadership, Dubai style.

GET OUT OF YOUR OFFICE

Monitoring, of course, isn't limited to the Al Maktoums. Wal-Mart founder Sam Walton famously described his management style as "management by walking and flying around." Others at Wal-Mart described it as "management by looking over your shoulder." I'm sure they didn't mean this as a compliment, but it begs the question, "Would Wal-Mart have become a success without it?" No!—the same as with Dubai. Wal-Mart enjoys a 20-year average return on equity of 33 percent, average sales growth of 35 percent, and incredible sales per square foot—50 percent better than the industry.[63]

"You've got to give folks responsibility, you've got to

trust them, and then you've got to check up on them," according to Walton.[64]

When leaders have the mind-set of making sure their teams succeed, then monitoring moves from inspection, which invokes resistance, to proactively ensuring success. Any boss can set annual Key Performance Indicators (KPIs) and then try to rely on twice-per-year performance reviews as a means to deliver them. But this is simply insufficient when it comes to monitoring for future success. Reactive, after-the-fact performance reviews are the antithesis of the type of leadership Sheikh Rashid was deploying when he drove around Dubai every morning after Fajr prayers. Effective monitoring happens in live time. It is more, much more, than a formal twice-a-year or once-a-quarter process. So what's the right frequency in your case?

Majid Al Futtaim, owner and operator of more than a dozen malls, including the Mall of the Emirates, walks his malls every single week. Surely, the owner of a multibillion-dollar business could justifiably kick his feet up on his desk and admire the view from his penthouse office. But Majid Al Futtaim is "hungry" to see the "shopping bag" test firsthand: How many bags are people carrying in their hands? Are they full? More this week than last week? What types of goods are people buying? This simple manual test is an economic indicator for how well the stores are turning over their inventory.

Some would argue, however, that walking the malls every week is really just too much for an owner. A few of his employees complained that whenever "the owner" (as he's affectionately called) came around, he would notice things that were out of place and redirect their focus.

"He shouldn't get so involved in the details of the business," moaned one of the senior managers, one of a dozen or so people in my Results Leader Program for senior executives. "We should be left alone to do the work we were hired to do; after all, we're the professionals that he hired to run his business."

"You're right!" another director agreed. "It's very distracting when he keeps giving us lists of what to focus on. So often he's involved in the tiniest details, like the bins being out of place or the fact that the planters were moved."

"Guys," said a senior Emirati director, "we shouldn't be upset that he's monitoring the malls. We should be upset that what he's finding, we should have found and corrected [ourselves]."

Al Futtaim's employees could have had it worse—much worse. In Dubai, as we've seen, it's common for monitoring to happen each day. Explaining what it's like to work closely with Sheikh Mohammed, Ahmed Bahrozyan, CEO of the Licensing Agency at Dubai's Road and Transport Authority, shared, "You have to always be on your toes; you never know when His Highness will show up."[65] Frankly, no one knows when it will happen—morning, noon, or night.

At least in the government sector, this type of "surprise" daily monitoring is often necessary to garner results. On May 22, 2013, Sheikh Mohammed gathered one thousand Dubai government employees and announced a two-year "Mobile Government" initiative (which was later rebranded as "Smart Government"). In other words, a new mission was handed down from the "field marshal" to the "troops." The vision was to provide better government services—to serve people wherever they were, at any time, via their smartphones.

Immediately after the announcement, the media was

flooded with the initiatives the various government entities were going to undertake. Headlines read, "Dubai Courts Targets 10,000 Suggestions or Ideas," "Dubai Trade Launches Its Mobile Strategy," and "Dubai SME Launches 'SeedApp' to Promote UAE's Transformation into m-government."

Then the announcements subsided and it looked like leaders had fallen back into the everyday routine of running their entities. After all, two years can seem like a long way off. But not to Sheikh Mohammed. He was determined to make sure everyone was focused on this transition and that they'd deliver by the deadline.

Marwan bin Ghalaita, CEO of one of Dubai's most important regulatory bodies, the Real Estate Regulatory Authority (RERA), recalled how one day he and the director general of the Land Department received an urgent call from the main floor. "His Highness is here!" said the receptionist, who, like the two men, was stunned by Sheikh Mohammed's unexpected appearance.

"Where is the archive department?" Sheikh Mohammed asked when he briskly walked into the Land Department building. He wasn't there to chat. He was there to monitor the progress "on the floor."

Rushing down eight flights of stairs to greet His Highness, the director general and bin Ghalaita arrived to hear Sheikh Mohammed ask the clerk at the archive desk, "Do you use paper?"

When he replied, "Um, yes sir," Sheikh Mohammed turned and walked away. He didn't even talk with the director general or bin Ghalaita. He simply left. His message was delivered loud and clear—keep smart government a priority. And they did!

For the government of the future to work 24/7, 365 days a year it would have to be paperless. So, rather than relying on progress updates or discussing status reports, Sheikh Mohammed went straight to the heart of the matter, in real time: Were the government departments using paper, or not?

Several months later, the exact same scenario unfolded. Sheikh Mohammed showed up to the Land Department office unannounced. He briskly made his way to the Archive Department as urgent calls went upstairs to the director general and bin Ghalaita informing them His Highness was there.

They rushed down the stairs right in time to hear, "Do you use paper?"

"No sir, we do not," was proudly said.

To which Sheikh Mohammed told everyone there, "Great job! Keep up the good work."

It is amazing how fast the news of monitoring spreads and the contagious effect it has. On May 23, 2015, two years later as promised, Sheikh Mohammed received formal reports saying that 96.3 percent of the 337 most important day-to-day governmental services had transitioned to smart platforms.[66]

MONITOR TO SHAPE BEHAVIOR

This approach to leading is highly disputed; many leaders argue that it's wrong to monitor this intensely. "Traditional" textbooks say leaders should give the vision or direction to their employees or teams, get their buy-in to the vision, and let them get after it—planning and executing. Reality, however, doesn't work like the textbooks read; obtaining results requires monitoring.

Another example that proves just how successful monitoring can be comes from one of Dubai's government departments, which—for better or worse—had an endemic culture of tardiness. (I'm leaving out the specific name of the government department, as well as its employees, to protect the guilty.)

Where is everyone? the director general wondered on his first day in his new post in 2004. He arrived eager to meet his new employees but very few were at their stations.

Slowly walking down the hallway toward his own office, a rather shocking and disappointing reality dawned on him: this was how the department behaved, every day. He felt like he had to do something. But what? A memo? A town hall address? Should he install a horn like the kind used in factories, the ones that signal shift changes and starting times?

Wrestling with what to do, his gut told him that punishing tardy employees wasn't the answer. As he thought about this, he focused on what mattered most to him—shaping the behavior that would eventually lead to the delivery of better results. To get future results and have a performance-based culture, he needed to start first with the employees' behavior.

Beginning the next morning, he greeted every employee as he or she arrived at the door. "Morning, how are you?" he'd ask, whether the employee walked in early, late, or right on time. What amazed me was how he restrained himself from lecturing the tardy employees right then and there. He merely said, "Morning, how are you?"

Of course, the employees knew they were late; they all knew the workday started at 7:30 a.m. But the culture accepted tardiness. That is, until the new boss began standing at the door and welcoming each employee. Each morning for two weeks, he repeated the routine. And each day, more of the employees got the point: be on time.

"I taught them discipline," recalls the director general. "I wasn't focused on results at first; rather, the behavior that would get the results." After just two weeks of monitoring, everyone was on time.

"After this I started gradually emphasizing goals and objectives. Then came developing people and systems to get even better."[67] This type of leadership did in fact change the employees' behavior for the better—much more effectively than any "punitive" policy would have done.

Says Sheikh Mohammed, who is notorious for frequently popping up at government offices, private businesses, and even restaurants and building sites: "I follow [Sheikh Rashid's] example. He would rise early and go alone to watch what was happening on each of his projects. I do the same. I watch. I read faces. I make decisions and I move fast. Full throttle."[68]

Setting the direction isn't enough: you have to make sure everyone's actually *doing* what's expected. There's no better way than proactively, informally monitoring to ensure progress is happening all the time. Proactive execution is the mantra of leadership success. Know what everyone's doing so you can help everyone succeed!

EIGHT

Circle of Loyalty

——Leadership Habit——
BE LOYAL IN ORDER TO GET LOYALTY

Within minutes of winning the right to host EXPO 2020, Sheikh Mohammed dedicated the victory to the UAE's president,[69] Sheikh Khalifa bin Zayed Al Nahyan, and its people. "We congratulate the nation, our president, and all people in the UAE on Dubai's winning bid to host the greatest exhibition in the world . . ." were the opening words of his celebratory comments.

Representatives from 116 (of 165) nations voted to select Dubai to host this mega-event, which lasts six months and occurs only once every five years. In 2020, twenty million visitors will converge on Dubai, experiencing its vision of being an "Al Wasl," or place were people can connect. It was the proverbial "cherry on top" for Dubai, signaling global recognition of Dubai's achievements, of building a world-class city in just a handful of decades. It is a remarkable testament to what ambitious leaders who stick to their strategy can accomplish. It would have been easy, therefore, for Sheikh Mohammed to take credit for winning the EXPO bid.

What caught my attention in Sheikh Mohammed's congratulatory note was its recognition of the president of the UAE, specifically giving the credit away. This comment represented more than the success of the night; it showed what I call "The Circle of Loyalty," which is a core leadership habit in Dubai. This is deeper than giving praise away; it is giving *credit* away.

A similar scene had repeated itself on September 18, 1990, when Atlanta won the right to host the 1996 Olympics—the twenty-fifth Olympiad, marking the hundredth anniversary of the modern games. Did Atlanta mayor Maynard Jackson congratulate then-US president George H. W. Bush? To the contrary, speaking from the Rose Garden at the White House, the president passed on the credit, acknowledging Mayor Jackson's and Atlanta's success. The victory was Atlanta's to savor—especially the team of volunteers who worked directly on the bid.

Understandably, you want credit for your successes. Naturally you want to be viewed as someone with a Midas touch. Yet, true leaders actually do the opposite. They give away credit for things that have gone well, specifically upward credit, and—perhaps more importantly—take the blame for things that turned out poorly. Whether it is an author finishing a new book and dedicating it to the president (as Sheikh Mohammed did after writing *My Vision*), a CEO achieving excellent results and dedicating them to Sheikh Mohammed, or winning a sports victory, you do not pin the badge on your chest. After winning top prize at HH The President of the UAE Endurance Cup equestrian race in 2015, local teenager Saeed Mohammed Khalifa Al Mehairi said, "I dedicate this win to Sheikh Mohammed, who was behind the success. He told me what to do—all I did was to implement his plan and strategy and it has worked."

Even traditional textbooks argue that leaders should give recognition to those who worked for the team's success. When you win, you should give the credit away! In Dubai this usually means giving "the trophy" to your boss, who may not have even worked for it.

"You don't take credit; you give it away," says Rick Pudner, former CEO of EmiratesNBD. This can be a paradoxical quality to Dubai's business culture: despite what others might perceive as a "brash" environment, in reality a refined humility is expected from leaders. Dubai is cautious about people who brag too much. This was evidenced while researching for this book. When I learned about a new feature at Emirates Airline during one of my interviews, I said, "You created that? I want to include this story in the book."

"You can tell the story," he said, "but please, just credit its success to the company. We don't like to draw attention to ourselves."

The "Circle of Loyalty" I mentioned before is the reason why leaders give the credit away. Just as in a real circle, where all points on a plane are equidistant from the center, in a circle of loyalty equal loyalty comes from everyone involved; all are interconnected. Dubai being good to its people, and the people being good to Dubai, motivates everyone to collectively want to contribute.

Given the strength of the habits in this book, it would be too easy for the circle to become imbalanced if this habit were ignored. For example, if you act as an autocrat; without the circle of loyalty habit, you may well become a dictator.

Additionally, the core of Dubai's strategy—creating an environment in which others can succeed—is in and of itself an act of loyalty. Without loyalty, you would be tempted to hoard for yourself the spoils of others' success. Loyalty is the tool that keeps all the *Leadership Dubai Style* habits in balance.

Keep in mind that loyalty isn't a positional guarantee. In tribal traditions, the people could and did rebel against the tribal chief, meaning that the tribal members were effectively deciding who was going to be the leader.

Following the economic crisis of 1928, Dubaian merchants, faced with high interest rates and increased international competition, felt they were losing the promise of their economic prosperity. At the beginning of the pearl season that fall, sixty boats—nearly all of them—stayed moored to the shore. Yet merchants still had to take out loans at exorbitant rates—36 percent—to be able to pay back the huge debts they owed to the Indian merchants who'd financed their boats.

Provoked by the Ruler's cousin, Sheikh Mana, they lashed out at Sheikh Saeed. In April 1929 he ceded his position to Sheikh Mana. (Assuming the election was more of a palace coup than an a declaration of allegiance, a few days later, the British sailed into Dubai's port, and clearly expressed that they wanted to restore the "will of the people." Sheikh Mana abdicated his rule, and the circle of loyalty was back in balance, as the majority of the people were still loyal to Sheikh Saeed and him to them.

The leader knows he must be loyal to his people or risk the people not returning the loyalty. And the people know they must be loyal as well. Knowing that loyalty may be temporal keeps everyone focused on building the circle. That being said, it's highly unlikely—I would assume even improbable—

in modern-day Dubai for the people to stand in opposition to the Ruler. Yet the habit of being loyal in order to get loyalty lives on, as it should.

PLEDGE OF ALLEGIANCE

When Sheikh Maktoum bin Butti died suddenly in 1852, his son, Sheikh Hasher bin Maktoum, was poised to take his place. Still only a teenager at the time, Sheikh Hasher was too inexperienced to lead this "new" Dubai and grapple with the demands of a burgeoning sheikhdom. So, the family rallied around Sheikh Saeed bin Butti, the brother of the deceased Ruler, giving him *bay'ah*.

Bay'ah, literally meaning "sale" or "commercial transaction" in Arabic, is a declaration of allegiance that is paid at the previous leader's burial, usually by tribal and community decision makers. Once they give their bay'ah, allegiance, their candidate's leadership is confirmed. "Bay'ah" may certainly only come from a few individuals, but in reality the individual giving bay'ah represents a group of people—the head of the family represents the whole family, the CEO represents the company, and the Sheikh the tribe. In this system, common people don't have to give their bay'ah. Rather, it is enough for them to be loyal—to commit themselves by obeying and submitting to the new Ruler, and not rebelling against him. In return for their bay'ah, the leader pledges his loyalty to his people.

Historically, giving bay'ah was a selection process led by the elders of the tribe. In modern times, it is assumed and normal that the people will honor the request of the deceased and give allegiance to the Crown Prince, knowing that he was groomed to be the Ruler. Still, this pledge of loyalty signals to the new Ruler what he should expect from his people.

Bay'ah is vastly different from the systems in place in many Western democracies. In England, for example, any person taking public or religious office is forced to swear allegiance to the monarch as Supreme Governor of the Church of England. Unlike the bay'ah system, where loyalty to the leader is given by choice, this "Oath of Supremacy" is demanded by the monarch. Failure to take this oath is grounds for treason. Similarly, in the United States, citizens pledge their allegiance to the United States Constitution, or the state, without receiving a circular pledge of loyalty in return.

In a corporate setting bay'ah would be the equivalent of employees pledging their loyalty to a new boss, sight unseen. This flies in the face of the "we'll wait and see approach," so common in business today. In this prevailing "ethos," employees may be loyal later, but not until that loyalty is "earned."

EQUALLY DEVOTED

In a highly functional circle of loyalty, you owe loyalty, and your employees owe it back. It is bidirectional. Think of it as two one-way streets, rather than a single two-way street. On two one-way streets, both parties focus on being loyal rather than receiving loyalty or "keeping score." Bidirectional loyalty between different people—for example, between employees and their employer—is the notion of the circle of loyalty. It is the basis of collaboration—working together.

When asked why she wanted to work in a semigovernment role, albeit the CEO of a major free zone and contributor to Dubai's economy, Amina Al Rustamani said, with a look of contentment in her eyes, "I'm serving my city and country."[70] Al Rustamani doesn't have to work for the government; she could easily work in the family business or not work at all. Yet she chooses to serve. To be loyal.

Loyalty makes you feel part of the system. Given the strong centralized leadership style in Dubai—the autocratic approach—the circle of loyalty is what gives the constant comfort that the leader is working for your best interest. Autocratic leadership without loyalty is tyrannical. With loyalty, this style of leadership becomes collaborative and caring.

This kind of loyalty means being devoted and deeply dedicated to somebody else, or even to a cause or an idea. It means showing real faithfulness, rather than being transactional—doing what you need to in order to get what you want—or transient, which amounts to temporal faithfulness. Dubai-style loyalty runs deep, in that it isn't merely a casual interest but a wholehearted commitment.

Mohammed Alabbar, CEO of Emaar Properties, experienced this special kind of loyalty when Sheikh Mohammed invited himself over for dinner one evening in 2007. That afternoon, Alabbar—as a proud father does—had casually shared with the Sheikh that his son, Rashid, had just returned to Dubai after graduating from university in the United States. That night, they'd be celebrating his achievement. When Sheikh Mohammed told him, "I will be there," Alabbar tried to talk the Sheikh out of it. "It's just a small, really small, dinner for family and friends," he said. Sheikh Mohammed would hear nothing of this. "You are a gift to me—and your son is also a gift to me because he is a gift to you."

Indeed Sheikh Mohammed did show up that night, but not for long: he didn't want to divert attention away from

Rashid. This was a win-win for both men: Sheikh Mohammed was able to demonstrate his loyalty, and Alabbar was rightly proud of the Ruler's visit. Both felt great as a result, and the dinner helped to deepen an already-close relationship.

This same kind of loyalty also presented itself in Sheikh Rashid's majlis. One night, shortly after Sheikh Mohammed had returned from Mons Officer Cadet School, a visitor suddenly became aggressive in his father's majlis. The person slammed the ground with his stick. Instinctively Sheikh Mohammed stood. This inappropriate and disrespectful behavior needed to stop.

Sheikh Rashid pulled his son back into his seat, making it clear that he should butt out. Afterward, he said to his son, "When I am there, I am in charge. And I will determine what happens." He knew that his son wanted the man to stop. "But [the man] had probably thought for a week about what he was going to say to me about his problem. So he got excited, and started banging his stick to emphasize his points."

"You know, sometimes you just have to listen to people," Sheikh Rashid continued. "You just have to accept them for what they are. That man wasn't being rude. He was simply being what he was. He had a grievance and was conveying it to me in the strongest possible way. Sometimes people have a reason for raising their voice. It doesn't always mean they are insulting you."[71]

The point was very clear: you are to remain loyal, even when you don't feel your people are. Concentrate on your "one-way street" of loyalty!

GIVE AWAY

It is customary for Dubaians to celebrate Accession Day—the anniversary of when a Ruler took office—by publishing wishes and greetings in the media and decorating the streets. During that day, the city becomes awash in receptions, parties, and parades, and the newspapers burst with full-page ads congratulating the Ruler.

On the anniversary of his accession, however—January 4—Sheikh Mohammed often chooses to redirect the celebrations to honor and thank certain underappreciated segments of society. One year he dedicated the day to mothers, another year to orphans, and another year to labor workers. He even dedicated one year to UAE president Sheikh Khalifa bin Zayed Al Nahyan, who obviously wasn't underappreciated, but he was deserving. The Sheikh's actions gave honor to everyone.

Unsurprisingly, when "common" people speak of Sheikh Mohammed, it is with endearment. Frankly, I've never heard people speak with such commitment to a leader, especially a leader whom most of the people have never met. Even the most "prominent" in Dubai's society, those who could theoretically operate as "lone wolves," make space for the Sheikh. Gerald Lawless, for example, makes it a point to go to the hotel anytime Sheikh Mohammed stops by for lunch. With a perfectly competent team in place to cater to His Highness's needs, Lawless' presence isn't requested, and maybe not even expected. Yet he makes these special trips because he wants to show respect, to show loyalty to the "big boss." Why else would the director general and bin Ghalaita rush down to welcome Sheikh Mohammed to the Land Department? It's a public demonstration of a wholehearted commitment.

Stories abound about Rulers giving away land and providing business opportunities to those who showed loyalty. Sheikh Rashid was known for supporting people who backed his plan for Dubai, often awarding contracts to those who fulfilled previous ones. All you had to do was perform to his expectations and he was glad to give you more work. You could argue that such practices gave certain people in Dubai an unfair competitive advantage. Maybe, but it highlights the point of being loyal to the people through giving away valuable resources.

When it comes to invoking eminent domain—claiming private property for public use—Dubai's leaders display a surprising sensitivity and sense of loyalty, often overcompensating for the act. When a letter shows up in someone's postbox outlining that a road is coming through the neighborhood and the government needs that person's home, the letter always contains an offer of cash compensation, new land, and the building of a new home or commercial building on that land. By Western standards, where only "just" compensation is paid, based on a home's "fair market value," cash, land, and the construction of a new home is an amazingly generous offer. Why do leaders do this, if they freely give tracts of land to the people to begin with? Loyalty! There's no other reason.

What surprised me most when learning of this practice was the reaction of most citizens. Often, they freely give part back to the government, refusing to take the full offer of cash compensation, land, and a house. In some cases citizens take the new land and compensation, but not the new building. Always they wholeheartedly give part of what the Ruler is offering them back to him. Again, this is an act of loyalty.

The circle of loyalty also shows up in the way Rulers and the people dealt with projects. When establishing the budget for a new project, Sheikh Rashid would set a price that was enough to cover the costs and also leave a profit. On occasion, however, the price was too low—a point that was only discovered deep into the project. According to biographer Graeme Wilson, "No one ever went back to Sheikh Rashid to ask for more money. The thought was that if you did the job well it would lead to more, so soaking up a small loss on one project was a modest sacrifice to make for more work."[72] Again, the circle of loyalty requires both parties—those awarding the projects and those delivering it—committing to each other.

Those who didn't support the strategy were encouraged to find a future elsewhere—sometimes moving trucks would suddenly show up at detractors' houses. Obviously it would be cumbersome today to send moving trucks to all who are here to consume rather than contribute—that is, expecting the benefits without being loyal—but the message remains the same. Be disloyal at your own risk.

"HERE IN DUBAI . . ."

I've never understood why it's so easy for "outsiders" to swoop in and complain about the way things are done here, beginning their sentences with "Here in Dubai . . .," inevitably followed by a put-down. At the macrolevel it's just plain rude. But on the practical level, because everyone who lives and works here is part of Dubai, all should be loyal. It's incredibly frustrating and insulting to hear these comments from outsiders who have made Dubai their temporary, or even permanent, home. If you don't like it here, the airplane that brought you to Dubai can take you right back to your utopia.

You may be thinking: "Wait—isn't everyone entitled to

his or her opinion?" Yes, but that doesn't remove the reality that your opinion often reveals the depth of your own loyalty.

Often, I interview prospective members of executive teams on behalf of CEOs, in order to discover what kind of leaders the prospects will be. CEOs want to know: "How will he or she lead? Who is this person as a leader?"

In one of these interviews, I listened as a prospective leader made continual references to "Here in Dubai . . ." He blamed allegedly bad suppliers in Dubai for his lack of "peak" performance, implying they weren't as bad anywhere else. He also had negative words about previous bosses, and how leaders at other companies in Dubai didn't know what they were doing strategically. Of course, this leader positioned himself as the white knight riding in on his horse to solve all the corporate world's ills. Where is loyalty in this attitude?

I wish this were the only time I experienced this type of disloyalty. Unfortunately, these instances are commonplace, showing up over dinners, in conversations between friends, in office hallways and cubicles, and even boardrooms. These demonstrations of supremacy and the willingness to blame something out of one's control are sneak peeks into someone's loyalty barometer.

"I'll teach them how to do it. . . ." My ears pricked at the words coming from the table next to mine, distracting me from reading over proofs of my last book, *10 Tips for Leading in the Middle East*. I was sitting on the seventy-first floor of the newly opened Marriott Marquis, the world's tallest hotel, enjoying a cigar while I did a final read-through before the book went off to the printers. *I'll teach them how to do it. . . .* The arrogance of those words stung deeply, as this first-time time visitor to Dubai thought he knew all the answers. I fought the urge to interrupt and direct the table's attention to the window in front of them, which featured a full view of Sheikh Zayed Road. "Should you teach them, or they you?" I longed to say. Clearly those business prospectors weren't a part of Dubai's "team."

The question I have for you is—if you work in a company and are part of the leadership team, and things aren't perfect, do you really see yourself as belonging to the team or separate from it? Are you loyal? Perhaps one of the ills discussed earlier describes your company. Do you tend to say the equivalent of "Here in . . . ," putting blame on others? All too often people are tempted to separate self-proclaimed "good" behavior from the group's actions.

Those of us living in Dubai should speak of "here in Dubai" as a badge of honor; we are accomplishing a lot and privileged that the Ruling Family allows us to contribute to their success. We should be loyal, and focus on the spirit of Sheikh Rashid's actions—to help people support the leaders' vision, to embrace life here. Remember that it takes two to create a circle of loyalty. In your own life—whether as a member of a family, a leader in a corporate corridor, or a role model for society—are you a billboard for loyalty?

Don't even try to escape team identity: you can't. As long as you are part of a team, a city, or a country, you are part of the "circle of loyalty." If you choose to live here in Dubai, then you are part of the emirate.

Sami Al Mufleh, CEO of Hills Advertising, one of Dubai's leading outdoor advertisers, is a prime example of someone who respects "the circle." Following the Global Financial Crisis of 2008, Al Mufleh had a choice: either he could keep the agency in Dubai, or he could pack up and go back to his hometown of Amman, Jordan, with the spoils. Would he be loyal to Dubai? Since opening in 2003, Hills Advertising had made millions by buying the rights to landmark outdoor advertising sites—from bridges to buildings—and then selling the advertising space to clients from Nokia to Dubai Holding, often clearing a 60 percent profit on each deal. Just prior to the Financial Crisis he was offered US $70million to sell the whole company. But he turned it down.

Faced with the decision to stay and be loyal or cash in and pack up, Al Mufleh had no doubt about which course to follow. "I believed in the future of the city, that it would work again," he told me. Since then, he chose to invest heavily in the city, spending AED150 million ($41million) on buying advertising space in three major locations in Dubai. Today his firm controls an estimated 65 percent of Dubai's outdoor advertising space.

When you are in a circle of loyalty, you remain loyal!

LOCUS OF LOYALTY

The locus of loyalty is among people, in the relationships that define life. Two friends demonstrate loyalty to each other. Husband and wife are loyal to each other. Even among colleagues and bosses loyalty is important, though unfortunately not always present. You should be loyal to your employees, your boss, and your customers, even your stakeholders. Oftentimes, as the following example demonstrates, bidirectional loyalty cuts across the barriers of "citizens" and "leaders."

One evening someone came to Sheikh Hamdan bin Rashid's majlis expressing concern about a friend. The friend had a very big family and a modest house. He claimed his friend was sad because his house didn't have appropriate rooms for his elder daughters. As the daughters matured, they needed private space and the house didn't have any. The man was ashamed, as he couldn't provide it.

After the majlis, Sheikh Hamdan bin Rashid jumped into his car to go and discreetly have a look. As he slowly drove down the road and came to the house, the gate was open. He peered in the driveway and then turned to his "right-hand" man sitting next to him.

"Remember this house," he said. "It belongs to Mr. So and So. Call him tomorrow morning, and say Sheikh Hamdan has heard the house isn't big enough." He emphasized "heard," not "seen," in order to preserve the owner's dignity and honor. "Don't tell him I saw it; just make sure he knows I heard." No one wants a Sheikh to see them suffering. Sheikh Hamdan continued, "Suggest to him: 'Why don't we build you a small addition to better be able to take care of your daughters'?"[73] And that is exactly what happened: Sheikh Hamdan's team built the addition to the house, making room for the man's daughters.

Frankly, the circle of loyalty is the basis for accountability. It is an essential element of why Dubai succeeds without the structure of a traditional democracy. The leaders and the people know the rewards of loyalty and the risk of not being. I call it practical democracy.

The leader knows he must be loyal or risk the people's not being loyal. And the people know they must be as well. The key is honoring your part, not focusing on if the other party is being loyal. Just be loyal!

Loyalty is the balance on the scales of an autocratic approach to leading. It is an essential element of why Dubai succeeds as a civil society without the structure of traditional democracy. Its also the "check" on the "underbelly" of the other habits in this book. Loyalty prevents an autocrat from becoming a dictator. Loyalty inspires you to create an environment for others to succeed, versus keeping all the spoils for yourself. And, as we'll see in the next chapter, loyalty is why you conduct a majlis—to consult with others in order to hear their perspectives.

Even if you have a position of power, followership isn't taken for granted in Dubai. Here, you have to be loyal in order to get loyalty—not the other way around. So, walk down your one-way street focused on giving loyalty, not getting it.

NINE

The Majlis

——Leadership Habit——
CONSULT TO BE INFORMED WHILE AVOIDING THE CONSENSUS LIMITATION

"Excuse me," the CEO interrupts energetically, stepping out of a meeting with his company's executive committee. "I need to take this call. It's the owner." Minutes later he's back, and the meeting is in full swing again. Suddenly, one of his team members grabs his phone in a way that indicates the owner is now calling *him*. You know that look: pride and surprise at the same time. Over the next fifteen minutes, the same scenario repeats itself three more times. By the end of the meeting, the owner has called five of his senior executives.

Is something wrong? An emergency that needs to be handled? Why in the world is the owner calling everyone?

The owner is practicing what I call the "virtual majlis." Literally, a majlis—"place of sitting" in Arabic—is a meeting room in a home, where guests, including neighbors, come together to discuss issues, air problems, and make decisions. Most homes in the Gulf have this room, so the head of the family can easily host guests. In reality, a majlis is more than the actual room. It's a "conceptual" as well as a physical gathering place for the community, in a sense similar to a popular European café or US coffee shop. It also functions as a formal legislative-like assembly, as the term has been used throughout this book.

The majlis historically helped leaders collect insights and stay current with what was happening in their constituencies, more so than formal reports or secondhand sources ever could. All throughout twentieth-century Dubai, daily morning meetings, also referred to as a *diwan*, between the heads of the merchant families and the head of the Ruling family gave the merchant elite powerful input in decision making. And it provided the Ruler with the information he needed to make wise decisions about the future of Dubai.

The evening majlis was more community centric. People would bring their needs and their grievances with them to the Sheikh. As he listened, usually solving their problems, he was getting a feel for what was happening in the community.

When the leader had an idea, he would ask those assembled, his trusted confidants, for their opinions. He'd then sit back and listen intently, watching as the debate moved from person to person. Oftentimes there'd be a friendly argument, with a whole range of opinions surfacing. Eventually the leader would lean forward and share his thoughts. No matter what happened, or who said what, the majlis was always a place of lively debate.

Tribal traditions are slowly fading away, with fewer people hosting a daily or weekly majlis than in the past. Now, instead of everyone congregating together in person, leaders conduct the idea of the majlis more informally: hence, the hasty CEO exits and the term virtual majlis—same practice, different medium.

No matter the format, the majlis is still the prime forum for leadership consultation in Dubai. Not consensus, but consultation. In the next sections, I'll deconstruct the difference between the two.

CONSENSUAL STATUS QUO

Consensus leadership is a group decision-making process where the agreement (consent) of all participants is mandatory. In many cases, people may give up their opinions for the sake of the group, even if the ultimate resolution isn't what they wanted. More often than not this ends up with "status quo" thinking—the consensus rarely chooses to break from tradition and do something bold.

This phenomenon is well documented in psychology, which tells us that the desire for harmony or conformity often results in irrational or dysfunctional decision making. People try to minimize conflict and reach consensus without critical evaluation of alternative viewpoints; they do this by actively suppressing dissenting viewpoints, and by isolating themselves from outside influences.

Working to achieve consensus can become highly political as each person lobbies to sway others to his or her point of view. A horrid example of this is the role of lobbying in a democracy. This controversial practice is in place to sway decision makers in favor of individual interests. Corporate hallways can begin to resemble the halls of Congress with all sorts of backroom political dealings.

When it doesn't become political, consensus-based leadership runs the risk of reaching the "least common denominator" as the point where everyone can agree. Sadly, this practice means the "brilliant" ideas stay hidden or are suppressed, giving the group the feeling that they're making great decisions, when in reality they're simply average. Consensus thinking gravitates toward safe decisions. While there's the off chance that "the people" can reach consensus on a brilliant idea, generally speaking grand ideas get stripped of their brilliance, as those ideas tend to be the most divisive ones.

In business, true consensus is nearly impossible to achieve. In other places in the Middle East, even across most of Asia and Africa, it is more common to find "faux" consensus where employees agree due to fear, respect, or cultural background. "Yes, boss!" and silence, not speaking up, are often mistaken for consensus. Such employees may grant their agreement, but fail to give true consensus.

The question is: What if the "consensus" obsession is wrong when it comes to ambitious results?

Frankly, if consensus leadership were practiced in Dubai, Dubai would still be an unknown town. I can't, for example, imagine in 1959 any "consultant" advising Dubai to launch any of its "grand" projects without having an off-setting revenue stream. Instead, I'm sure he or she would have tried to "please everyone" and "play it safe." Nor could I imagine Jebel Ali ever becoming a reality: remember that "the people" went to Sheikh Mohammed hoping he could talk his father out of building it. The consensus said, "Don't do it."

Luckily, though, this kind of "democratic leadership" is far from leading Dubai style. From other people's perspectives, many—probably most—of the decisions that created Dubai, into what we know it as today, were anything but safe.

CONSULTATIVE LEADERSHIP

Consensus is far from what happens in the majlis. Here, the host practices consultative leadership, where the opinion of others is sought, and closely listened to, but where the final decision always resides with the leader. As the leader, you act on what you feel is the best resolution after being informed on an issue.

Oftentimes consensus is confused with consultation. They are very different. As I pointed out earlier, consensus leadership, a group decision-making process where everyone must agree, easily results in compromise for compromise's sake. This is far from the majlis approach, which says that you should hear from those affected, but aren't bound by consent. The majlis style of leadership is an ideal picture of consultative leadership. It is seeking the public's input on matters affecting them. Those most affected by a decision have the most say, while those who are least affected have the least say.

The consultative leader wants to hear what others have to say; knowing that otherwise he is in a vacuum. Yet, he retains the right to make the final decision. After getting the input from those that will be affected, that is when you weigh the alternatives and make the final decision.

The "Mohammed bin Rashid Media Majlis"—Dubai's version of a reverse press conference—emanates from the Sheikh's strong belief in the importance of listening to the views, thoughts, and suggestions of media persons, whether from the UAE or from other Arab and foreign countries. In a typical "Media Majlis," Sheikh Mohammed will keenly listen to others' perspectives. He never wastes an opportunity to hear what people have to say.

Dubai-based businessman Mohammed Al Naboodah

says: "[The majlis] is a creative environment, in which people are allowed to speak freely. Sheikh Mohammed places no barriers on what can be said. It is this open atmosphere that cultivates a genuine, open debate. He challenges people to think and perform beyond the limit of the capabilities that they themselves believe they have. This brings out the best in people."[74]

The "majlis effect" demonstrates a type of maturity: as we've learned, majlis leaders willingly listen to others, include others, and seek their opinion. Public input is highly valued as a means to enrich debates and seek solutions to the many problems of society.

Circling back to the beginning of this chapter, the owner who called everyone at the meeting was simply trying to know what each person thought. He was collecting information. Make no mistake about this: he wasn't trying to build consensus; rather, he wanted to understand their perspective—what their thoughts were. Only after listening to what each had to say, would he decide on the issue.

If you want to practice "majlis-style" leadership, keep in mind that while you hold positional authority—autocracy—you still have to listen and take on board the opinions of those being led. Listen, understand, think about the issue, and then decide on a course of action. That is leadership, Dubai style.

As the previous examples demonstrate, the majlis style of leadership is very much alive in Dubai's business culture, even if only a few families still host daily physical majlis. This can be very frustrating for Western leaders, who think they were brought in to lead with full authority. Repeatedly I hear, "I don't think the owner of my company trusts me." When I ask, "Why do you feel this way?" the answer is often, "He calls my peers, my direct reports, and his friends, and asks them all the same questions he asked me." Thinking the owner is challenging him, the imported leader gets very angry. "I can't take this!" the CEO of one of the major family businesses told me a couple of years ago. "If he's going to keep seeking opinions from my team, then he can lead his own company." If you're brought in to lead here, you must know that consultation and seeking a broad range of opinions is very much a part of the leadership culture, and is in keeping with the spirit of the majlis. In other words, don't take things so personally when the owner of your company disrupts your meetings.

LISTEN TO CONVINCE

Apart from having to weather difficult questions, the most challenging part of "the majlis" habit for leaders is that the majlis must work in concert with the circle of loyalty. After listening to your team, for example, you may be convinced of a direction that they aren't. You then decide that your path is correct. Now you have a choice: You can boldly declare, "*Ana mudir* (I am the boss)! So, get on with what I said." Or you can win the people over to your idea. The latter is what you should do, even though it is the much harder work of leading, for it builds—and tests—the circle of loyalty.

The business context is hierarchal and consultative at the same time. The result is that consultation can shape decision-making processes in significant ways. Rarely would the Ruler decide in utter contradiction to the voice of the majlis. But that doesn't mean that the voice of the majority rules. The leader is to act in the best interest of all, which is vastly different than in accordance with suggestions.

A good example of soliciting this kind of loyalty comes from what happened just before Dubai launched its Strategic Plan of 2015. The plan centered around five pillars. Dubai would:

1. Become a global and multicultural city that wouldn't discriminate about who it would welcome
2. Serve as a catalyst for positive change in the region
3. Become a center for innovation
4. Be efficient, speedy, and transparent in executing projects, and
5. Be a globally responsible investor that also extends itself philanthropically to help disadvantaged people everywhere, by providing them with the essential means to lead dignified lives.

Obviously this is a solid, well-thought-out plan, impressive in scope. But city leaders wanted more: they thought they could do better. So, they presented the plan to a wide segment of the population: business leaders, developers, financiers, government leaders, and ordinary citizens. The leaders wanted to hear what others thought, how they would respond when working to implement the plan. This input was ultimately used to shape the implementation plan of the strategy—not so much the direction, just the execution.

Your own business decisions should be obtained through counsel and consultation with the ranks on the things they need to give input on, not "unanimous faux" or "common denominator" consent. Just as in a family majlis, you need to be inclusive in your leadership. You should involve those affected by a decision, largely to make sure you accurately understand others' perspectives. Once you have consulted with others, only then is it time to decide and act. Only then can you build trust and loyalty.

When you know what is right, pursue it. But be sure you're informed and really know what is right, and that your decision isn't based merely on what you want.

STAY CLOSE

Physical proximity is an added advantage of the majlis. The very nature of the Sheikhs' majlis brought the leaders together every day, sometimes even twice a day. People who encounter each one another more frequently tend to develop stronger relationships. There is no doubt in my mind that the physical proximity granted by the majlis supported the speedy progress of Dubai—information was readily available, decisions were made on the spot, and community behavior was easily shaped. There were no barriers to communication; it was face to face every day.

The physical proximity advantage gained by the majlis contradicts the latest management teachings, which say that being close to one another is neither feasible nor essential.[75] But it is! Following the tragic 9/11 attacks in New York, then mayor Rudy Giuliani credited his team's success to the fact that "most mornings, most weekday mornings when I was the mayor . . . would start with an 8:00 a.m. meeting, either at City Hall or Gracie Mansion, depending on what the other events of the day were."[76] He pulled his top lieutenants together to discuss events every morning for eight years. Why? To consult with them and be informed. He had a New York City "majlis." Physical proximity matters if you want to achieve remarkable results. What better way to accomplish it than coming together every day?

It is very important to keep in mind that consultation isn't just about ideas; it's for the purpose of fulfilling the strategy. Sheikhs Rashid and Mohammed focused everyone on achieving a goal after each in their respective eras decided what he wanted. They were not asking people for their opinions on the direction of the city; they were seeking input on "how" to achieve the direction. Both were, at the end of the day, persuasive leaders who knew how to cajole others in the "right" way.

If I could say one thing about this leadership concept, I'd say, "Listen!" Give people the chance to share what's on their minds, and truly hear what they're saying. Know where they're coming from and understand. You cannot act in a void, separate from the people. But remember that consulting doesn't mean abdicating authority to the hands of your followers. It is instead a wise way to stay informed. When you're ready to make a move, make sure you base your decision on your purpose and strategy.

TEN

Don't Panic

——Leadership Habit——
BE BRAVE TO MAXIMIZE BUBBLES
AND SPRINT AWAY FROM CRISES

During the 1920s, the final day of pearling season was traditionally a day of great joy and celebration in the Gulf. Every fall, families would gather around the port, eagerly awaiting the safe return of their men, who'd been pearling at sea for six long months. As they heard the men's chants booming from their approaching boats, the families would rush to the beachfront to celebrate. But not in the fall of 1928: only gloom greeted the pearl divers in Dubai, as a perfect storm had settled over the industry they were all dependent on.

That summer, while the pearling fleet was at sea, a cheap alternative from Japan called "cultured pearls" had poured into the international markets, effectively wiping out the "natural pearl" industry in one fell swoop. Natural pearls are formed by nature, in response to an attack by a fish or other damaging event. In trying to heal itself, the oyster secretes a smooth, hard surface called nacre, forming a cyst around the irritant. After two to three years of depositing layer upon layer of nacre over the irritant, the oyster survives and a beautiful pearl is formed. Natural pearls are formed more or less by chance, making them so rare and expensive during the 1920s that they were reserved only for the aristocratic class.

By contrast, "cultured pearls" are human creations formed by artificially inserting a tissue graft from a donor oyster, on which a pearl sac forms, effectively replicating the natural process. In 1916, Japanese biologist Tokichi Nishikawa was granted the patent; a dozen years later, the first commercial crop of pearls was successfully produced, changing the industry and Dubai forever. Today, more than 99 percent of all pearls sold worldwide are cultured.

In 1928, the effect on Dubai was immediate and catastrophic. Fashion houses failed to arrive for the end-of-season buying period when the pearlers made their annual haul. With no sales in November 1928, there was no payment of salaries and no money to repay the "loan sharks"—those who provided money for the pearlers to buy more boats and employ more men. In previous years, Dubai's pearling industry had grown aggressively with the help of borrowed funds from India, leading Dubai deep into debt. Crews were typically paid half their salaries on departure—borrowed from moneylenders at a high rate of interest—and the second half on return after six months away.

Now, boat owners were immediately made bankrupt and 75 percent of liquidity from the market was gone. It was an economic shutdown! Pearling had formed the backbone of the Gulf economy and, during the early years of the 1900s, accounted for a whopping 95 percent of the area's economic activity. An unforeseen perfect storm settled over Dubai exactly one year before the Great Depression cast its gloomy shadow over the world.

Unfortunately, the Pearling Crisis was the first of many for Dubai. In this chapter, I'll share Dubai-style secrets for dealing with even the most crippling crises, so you and your organization can emerge stronger and wiser each time.

Crises come and crises go, so don't panic. Stick with your strategy, weather your storm, and get stronger.

PLAYING WITH BUBBLES

November 2008 was eerily similar to November 1928. Just as the world's largest shopping mall, Dubai Mall, was getting ready to throw open its doors, a disturbing reality started to work its way into boardrooms. The city would have no protection from the Global Financial Crisis.

The "bubble" had burst!

During the wild growth years leading up to 2008, a "property bubble" had formed in the system. Bubbles are a market dynamic where trade in high volumes and prices are considerably at variance with intrinsic values. This means that asset prices appear to be based on implausible or inconsistent views about the future. Prices in an economic bubble can fluctuate erratically, and become impossible to predict from supply and demand alone. Eventually, a correction sets in and the prices readjust, usually in the form of a sudden drop in prices—that is, the bursting of the bubble.

When you have a boom, you will have speculators. We all have a bit of greed in us. We all want to make a little bit more. In Dubai, the rapid increases in real estate valuations reached unsustainable levels despite the government's attempts to cool the market. When liquidity dried up, so did the market, rapidly declining in line with property bubbles that were popping up around the world.

When I think of the impending property bubble of 2008, I'm reminded of a dinner conversation I heard about, just after the Iraqi invasion of Kuwait in 1990. Reportedly, journalist Bikram Vohra was engaged in a discussion about the dramatic growth Dubai was experiencing at that time. At one point in the conversation a fellow diner said, "Yes, but for how long? The bubble will burst one day."

Vohra supposedly replied, "Bubbles always burst, but maybe Dubai will just dig into its bag, pull out more soapy water, and make another bubble and another and another and another ad infinitum."[77]

Vohra's imagery calls to mind the childhood game of making bubbles, which I think is actually called "bubbles." (In our household we say, "Let's go out in the garden and play bubbles!") My kids, as did I, love to go out into the garden with their bottle of soapy water, dip their stick into it, wave it in the air, and make bubbles.

Can you imagine someone saying to my kids, "You better be very careful—that bubble you're about to make will burst!"? Instead of putting our soapy sticks down and taking them inside, we—kids and adults—work harder to create the longest-lasting bubble. Those who can't create bubbles on their own aimlessly run around the yard chasing after the kids' bubbles, just like speculators who come into a market trying to "catch a break" and make a buck.

Everyone knows the bubbles will dissipate at some point, but they work to enjoy them for as long as they last. When the inevitable happens, the kids learn what caused a bubble to burst and work to make a bigger and longer-lasting bubble next time. One that will make them proudly say, "Look at that bubble!" Dubai-style leadership isn't about being afraid of bubbles; it's about learning how to reproduce growth. In other words, taking risks when the times are good allows for hyper-growth. Instead of focusing on avoiding a bubble, Dubai knows to grow when it can. History tells us that busts are always followed by recovery.

Life without bubbles would be quite boring. Instead of fighting bubbles, let's enjoy them and try to make them last as long as possible.

NEVER WASTE A CRISIS

Following the Pearling Crisis of 1928, local merchants begged young Sheikh Rashid for help. "What are we going to do now?" they wailed. Though his father, Sheikh Saeed, was still the Ruler of Dubai, the community recognized Sheikh Rashid's leadership ability. Admittedly, he had a lot on his shoulders.

"What are we good at?" the Sheikh wondered out loud. Dubai had nothing. And then a community member called out an answer: "Pearls!" Sheikh Rashid thought for a moment. "You mean the sea . . . Then, that's it!"

The Pearling Crisis left Dubai no other option than to return to the sea to survive, but not for pearl harvesting—to fish. Fishing would employ men, provide food for the families, and produce a product for export. Although he had never been involved in the fishing industry, Sheikh Rashid decided to lead his citizens back to the sea. This was his answer.

Sheikh Saeed (Ruler at the time) invested the limited state funds in new fishing boats, but needed more if he was going to move forward. So, he did what many future leaders would do: he borrowed his way out of the crisis, tapping into the bank accounts of wealthy merchants along the Arabian Sea Coast. That way, he could invest in boats and employ people.

You may think this was irresponsible, but remember: when you have a hunger of need you're willing to do what the satisfied man thinks imprudent. Dubai survived the Pearling Crisis and the people didn't starve. It became the major trading port on the Arabian Peninsula, and despite the recession, its diverse souq retained a level of wealth envied by its neighbors.[78] So, Sheikh Saeed moved ahead.

After putting all their personal assets at the disposal of the city, the Ruling family further diversified the economy by selling rights for oil exploration, the first of the Trucial Rulers to do so. With the discovery of oil in nearby Iraq, Bahrain, Kuwait, and Saudi Arabia, Sheikh Saeed banked on Dubai also finding oil, and looked to the future revenue it would earn. By doing so the Sheikh acted three decades, a generation, ahead of time. By the late 1930s, financial instability had settled down and attention shifted firmly to the future, to the inevitable progress that lay ahead.

That is what you should do in a time of crisis: stay focused on the future and move forward. A crisis isn't the time to stop; it's the time to work even harder. Frankly, a crisis is your real opportunity for success, because what you do at the low points will determine your future trajectory.

This may sound counterintuitive, but a crisis offers you the best opportunity to change the game in your favor, with new products or services that will grow market share. Many people look at a crisis as something to get through, until they can go back to business as usual. But "business as usual" never returns because markets are irrevocably changed after a crisis. Why not create changes that move the market in your favor, instead of waiting and reacting to the changes as they take place?

This principle is wrapped up in the question: Do you respond by waiting on uncertainty to stabilize? In other words, by focusing on merely surviving? Or do you stay focused on your strategy—the future? Or what I label "succeeding"? Are you survival or success focused?

In the mid-1980s, Dubai, along with the other GCC countries, experienced a vicious economic contraction as a result of the Iran-Iraq War and a downturn in oil prices. Oil exports were severely interrupted, and the UAE was forced to invest billions in their armed forces to defend itself and guarantee security. As the markets slowed and liquidity dried up, countless private-sector companies inevitably folded under the pressure.

With its heavy dependence on commerce, Dubai suffered its first sustained recession since the Pearling Crisis. Instead of panicking, what did its leaders do? They stuck with the strategy—growth—and focused more intensely on creating an environment where others could succeed. As we saw earlier, it was in the midst of this crisis that Dubai launched its flagship carrier, Emirates Airline. Not only would greater government investment boost the economy, but it would also lay the foundation for Dubai after the current period of uncertainty.

A few years later, when Iraq invaded Kuwait in 1990, shipping froze in the northern ports of the Gulf. As insurance risks skyrocketed, ports in this area quickly became defunct. Dubai shrewdly responded to its neighbors' dilemma by absorbing the insurance risk. The city branded itself as a trans-shipping portal, transferring cargo from larger international ships to smaller local vessels for distribution. Combined, this enabled Dubai's ports to keep functioning during the war and thus keep Dubai's lifeline open; more than that, it positioned the ports for future growth.

As stated before, times of crisis test your courage and commitment. During a crisis you either stay focused and get stronger or sit on the sidelines and wait. Never waste a good crisis. It provides you with the platform to get things done that were required anyway, and offers a sense of urgency to accelerate their implementation.

SPEED AHEAD

Dubai faced its next major crisis following the 9/11 attacks in America. Again, where others saw calamity, in the midst of one of the worst years for the aviation industry, Dubai saw an opportunity. Stunning the world, Emirates Airline announced in November 2001 that it had placed a $15 billion order for fifteen A380s, eight A340-600s, three A330s, and twenty-five Boeing 777s. Most people were critical, saying Dubai should take note of the airlines that had been forced to declare bankruptcy. The analysts and journalists felt Dubai was taking unrestrained risk. Yet leading Dubai style looks to the future, not immediate circumstances. In actuality, Dubai took a calculated risk. Leaders knew that the situation following 9/11 was temporary; the market would, of course, recover.

Shortly after that disastrous attack, Sheik Ahmed bin Saeed sent a note to Emirates Airline staff encouraging them to stay focused. While the world was reeling, he knew that recovery was coming and wanted Emirates to be ready.

Almost a decade later, Emirates Airline again shocked the global aviation world, this time by announcing a 52 percent surge in annual profits to $1.5 billion.[79] You can trace this success right back to the record aircraft order placed in November 2001, a move that was clearly very beneficial as part of the airline's general expansion strategy.

In 2009, listening to the economists and coffee-shop theorists spout on about what Dubai should've done after the Global Financial Crisis, I learned an important element of this habit—you can work to avoid future crises or work to achieve as much as possible during times of upheaval. The vast majority of commentators, from professional journalists to economists to "average Joes," believed that Dubai should have done more to avoid—and then ameliorate—the crisis: temper its ambition, use more prudent short-term cash management. . .These "experts" seemed to have all the answers. Yet had Dubai followed their advice, we wouldn't have the city that it is today.

I'm not suggesting being imprudent and taking a "Vegas"-style approach. But you should try to achieve as much as possible during crises. The period following a crisis isn't the time to sit still: it's the time to sprint.

Maybe you want to call it overreaching, or perhaps taking a big, big risk. But each of Dubai's history markers shows the success of acting today, for tomorrow.

Taking risks when times are good allows for hyper-growth. Sure, they make your dark days tough, but you'll soon be at new heights, ones you couldn't achieve if you focused on avoiding a bubble. Sheikh Mohammed is never content to take small steps when giant ones will do. He might never again have the opportunity to do what he can today, tomorrow. Instead of focusing on avoiding a bubble, learn from Dubai: grow when you can.

The lessons Dubai has learned from its various crises are different than the textbooks would have us learn. The theoretical perspective says that crises make you more prudent and conservative, guiding you to take a cautionary view of the future. But take a moment to think about it: If you subscribe to the theory that leaders shouldn't overreach, at what point in the past would you have done something differently, if you were leading Dubai? Would you have refused to overbuild the infrastructure in 1959 when Dubai had minimal revenue sources? Would you have hesitated to create Emirates Airline in the mid-80s crisis? When funds were easy to borrow in the early 2000s, would you have opted not to borrow aggressively in order to build rapidly?

The leadership habit mentioned here teaches us that busts are followed by recovery and should give you confidence that days of growth will come again. Dubai has always recovered, emerging better than it was before. Dubai gets stronger. The focus—either in the bubble or bust—always remains on growth.

As a leader, you can "play it safe"—get rid of bubbles, yet strip yourself of growth—or you can learn to live with bubbles and see how long you can make them last. As we know, when bubbles burst there are consequences that none of us like. But after a bit of effort, we can regenerate growth and make bubble after bubble, just like children do when they "magically" create bigger and longer-lasting bubbles with their wands.

Do nothing and the future is determined. Take a risk and it may be different.

GIVE COMFORT AND CONFIDENCE

When speaking of the 2008 Global Financial Crisis and its reverberating shocks, now with a sense of relief that it had passed, Mohamed Alabbar said, "I used to spend a lot of time around His Highness at that time. I needed the psychological support. He is like a rock. He does not move. He is someone you can lean on."[80]

No one needed a rock more than Alabbar. In 2008, Alabbar's company, Emaar, was a year away from opening the Burj Khalifa, which was in the final stage of development after five tireless years of construction. While critics boldly and publicly questioned his plans, Alabbar made a behind-the-scenes decision to continue on with the project. "[I]t was the right time that we say 'Come on, let's move on. We need some good news.' Was it challenging? Of course it was challenging. Of course there were a lot of unknowns on how long this disaster would last worldwide." Yet he remained loyal, putting a priority on boosting the confidence of his team—and the city. Despite being in the eye of the storm, Emaar continued on with their plans, opening the Burj Khalifa in the middle of the crisis on January 4, 2010.

Alabbar continues, "Nobody stopped. There was no long-term debating of what should be done. We just got on with it. And the reality is that Dubai has come out of the crisis much, much stronger." As the world's tallest building, the Burj Khalifa today is a thriving landmark in Dubai, and a continual source of inspiration to the broader business community.

Another of Dubai's leading businessmen, Osman Sultan, CEO of du, recalled a moving incident from those days. Sitting in the comfort of his office overlooking the completed Palm Island, Sultan remembered going to his chairman, Ahmad bin Byat, saying, "I know you are under lots of pressure," being sensitive to the impact of the Financial Crisis. Instead of weighing Sultan down with his problems, the chairman simply said, "Tell me what you want me to do to support you."[81] When times are tough, give your people confidence. Give comfort to your people in the midst of a crisis. Don't panic! Others are looking to you for a signal as to how they should feel. When you are calm and centered, it sends the signal to stay steady ahead. Be the rock that your people can lean on.

A key to being this kind of leader is believing in the inevitability of another growth window. While Dubai was working its way through the aftermath of the Global Financial Crisis, picking up the pieces of its deflated property market, its leaders were busy in the background preparing their bid for EXPO 2020. So what if Dubai was actually cash strapped? EXPO fever made the businesses in Dubai feel secure, giving their owners a sense of confidence about the future. Seeing that the leaders were planning and investing made everyone hopeful. The leaders' confidence radiated throughout the city, giving everyone the courage to act, to grow. Even while there was an immediate calamity demanding their attention, it didn't dissuade them from planning a decade into the future.

Leadership Dubai style takes risks, even risks that others may not understand or agree with. A hunger of need requires a higher-than-average risk tolerance. Reach as far as you can, when you can.

Mohammed Al Shaibani, director general of the Ruler's Court,[82] says about the years between 2003 and 2008: "We rode that wave well. We used the boom to build infrastructure. We expanded the airport, we did the train [Dubai's metro], we did a state-of-the-art road network, [and] we invested huge money in electricity. . . . If it weren't for that business boom we couldn't have done what we did. So I think we did fantastically well."[83]

The lesson here? Don't be afraid of crises: doing so will only strip you of your growth potential. Accept that crises are an inevitable reality, so instead of working to avoid them at all costs, maximize the growth times and minimize the post-crises moments by charging ahead toward growth. This leadership habit is a sprint—into and out of a crisis. It is never a casual stroll.

ELEVEN

Better

——Leadership Habit——
DON'T ACCEPT "GOOD ENOUGH" AS GOOD ENOUGH

In 2002, there were only four buildings in the world with more than one hundred floors. So when Mohamed Alabbar approached Sheikh Mohammed proudly displaying plans to build a ninety-story tower to anchor what would become the Downtown Dubai development, he was sure the Sheikh would be pleased.

"Ninety is a waste of time!" Sheikh Mohammed instead exclaimed, not even taking the time to study Alabbar's plans. "What is the tallest?"

"The tallest is one hundred plus," said Alabbar, meekly.

Immediately, His Highness got up and walked out of the meeting. It lasted mere minutes.

In shock, Alabbar chased him down the hall. "So should we start construction?" he asked.

"I think you should try harder," Sheikh Mohammed told him.

Alabbar got it. What he was proposing was definitely respectable by most standards. But for Sheikh Mohammed "good enough" isn't good enough. Alabbar's plans were good, but they could be better. Walking away from the incident, he thought, *I need to be that person who can think as big as Sheikh Mohammed can think.*

Over the next three months, Alabbar did a comparison of the tallest buildings in the world and created a new plan. When he was finished he again went to see Sheikh Mohammed.

"I promise you, I won't let you down this time," Alabbar said.

"Are you sure?" Sheikh Mohammed asked.

"I promise!"

Sheikh Mohammed studied the plans, asking just one question: "How high?"

Alabbar was ready. "This building will be 40 percent taller than anything else that has ever been built."

"When will the cranes be on-site?" asked His Highness.

Today, the Burj Khalifa, known as the Burj Dubai before its inauguration, is the tallest man-made structure in the world, standing at 829.8 meters (2,722 feet), or more than 160 stories. It is the centerpiece of Downtown Dubai, a two-square-kilometer (nearly 500-acre) development that's home to several other important landmarks, including Dubai Mall and Dubai Fountain, both of which are also the largest of their kind in the world. Dubai Mall attracts eighty million visitors per year, making it the world's most visited lifestyle destination and the world's most popular tourist destination, ahead of Disney World's Magic Kingdom, Paris's Eiffel Tower, New York's Times Square, even New York City itself.[84]

MORE THAN GOOD ENOUGH

Building the Burj Khalifa pushed everyone to be better. Physically speaking, everything—from the pumping of the concrete, to the installation of the elevator systems, to the overall project engineering—had to be better. Since no similar structure had ever been built before, no one could merely copy what had already been done.

Conceptually speaking, the idea of the Burj Khalifa was also built on "better." Going back to the strategy of Dubai being a place where people can come, connect, and succeed, Dubai needed to further develop its service and tourism sectors, to lessen its dependence on oil revenues. According to officials, projects like the Burj Khalifa are necessary in order to garner more international recognition, to entice more people to come to Dubai—in other words, to make Dubai better. Sheikh Mohammed wanted to put Dubai on the map with something really sensational!

Good enough simply isn't good enough in Dubai. Leading Dubai style is a constant pursuit of being better, actually being the best. I wonder how many leaders would have allowed a "Mohamed Alabbar" to proceed with his original plans to build a ninety-story building when they should have pushed him for better. Or worse, would have found every reason why he should not even build a tower.

Famed psychologists Paul Fitts and Michael Posner,[85] expert researchers in the area of performance improvement, argue that most people settle for things being just "good enough." Fitts and Posner discovered that most of us pass through three distinct stages when acquiring a skill, a behavior, or an attitude (the three core ingredients of performance). During the first stage, we intellectualize the task and discover new ways to accomplish it more proficiently. We're very aware of what we're doing, and are concentrating on improving. In effect, stage one is the "practice" stage. But practice doesn't make perfect. My dad used to always correct the phrase "Practice makes perfect," saying, "Perfect practice makes perfect." Practicing something only makes you better in the way you're doing it. If you're making a mistake while practicing, you will become great at making this same mistake.

When you improve—get better at something—you move into Fitts and Posner's second stage, learning by simply doing, not thinking. During the second stage, we concentrate less, as we're actually getting better at carrying out a task. We thus make fewer errors and generally become more efficient.

That may sound like the ideal situation, as if you've mastered what you're doing, until you realize progress isn't being made. In this stage, it's easy to go into autonomous autopilot. But in order to break automatic action and kick-start progress, you've got to go back to the first stage of learning from time to time. So you need to go back to stage one again.

Then comes the third stage, where we figure that we've gotten as good as we feel we need to get at a specific task, skill, or behavior. Thereafter, we basically run on autopilot, thinking that we're as good as we need to be. We stagnate, not even realizing we've stopped trying to be as good as we *can* be. To use a practical example, most people in Dubai drive everyday, yet unless they're professional drivers, it's likely that their ability to drive will get only incrementally better—and that may be a stretch. The same holds true for the way we lead. We do it everyday, and most likely we do it as we have for years. Instead of getting better, the law of inertia says if we've settled for good enough, we're still just good enough.

The business implication of this is that performance also stagnates. Your employees begin to feel they're performing as well as they need to. And you may even accept this as reality. To gain improvement, you need to keep returning to stage one. That's the hard part in all this. According to Fitts and Posner, when you receive feedback from others you must comprehend, process, evaluate, and chose what you will do based upon what was shared. While this sounds like common sense, it is not common practice. Most people stop thinking about what they're doing and how they're doing it. They lack the motivation to try new ways to accomplish their task more proficiently. Leading Dubai style is staying consciously aware that you can get better, and then pursuing that improvement.

When asked about where he got the idea for the Burj Khalifa, Alabbar shared, "There is a continuous search in my head. I am always thinking. I am always searching."[86] Better starts in the mind, having an idea.

The older we get, the harder it is to get better. This is because we've been doing it "our way" for most of our lives. Over time learning slows down and progress gets harder. This explains why most people never progress beyond "good is good enough." They get stuck at doing something the way they've already learned how to do it.

When he was just starting out as a serious equestrian owner, Sheikh Mohammed could've easily "stagnated" at stage two or three. By 1979, only two years after his first victory, the Sheikh had already amassed eleven wins. By many standards he was off to a fantastic start, and I'm sure advice dribbled in to stick with what he was doing, the way he was doing it. But that wasn't good enough for Sheikh Mohammed. So he decided to sneak into Keeneland.

Keeneland is the world's largest thoroughbred auction house, located in Lexington, Kentucky. Keeneland is where you go to buy a winner—horses sold at Keeneland frequently go on to win the Breeders' Cup World Championship, the Kentucky Derby, Preakness, and other top races.

Before he entered the auction house, Sheikh Mohammed had convinced himself that it would be better to attend without anyone knowing he was there, so he could freely observe his surroundings. Having grown up around horses as a young boy, he'd learned from his father what to look for in a thoroughbred. Yet he wanted to absorb the theories on this from within the industry, from the ground up. So, returning to "stage one," he decided to sneak into Keeneland with the intention of learning and getting better on his own.

And get better he did. Thanks to his persistence and willingness to "go back to the drawing board," Sheikh Mohammed is now one of the leading horsemen in the world. To give just one example, Dubai Millennium—his personal favorite and one of his greatest horses—won nine of his ten races, including a stunning victory in the world's richest race, Dubai's World Cup. Held annually on the last Saturday of March, this thoroughbred horse race is coveted for its $30 million in prize money, with the finale carrying a cash payout of $10 million.

Have you maxed out your potential? Can you be any better?

Summarizing what it was like to work in Dubai, Raja Trad, Leo Burnett's CEO for the Middle East and Africa, and resident of Dubai since 1991, shares, "Whenever they told Sheikh Mohammed how long something would take, he divided it in half. If you say ten, then he would say do it in five."[87] And then you'd do what it took to make that happen.

DELIBERATE PRACTICE

Thinking about this idea of "good enough" made me wonder, *What specifically makes Dubai what it is and allows it to excel beyond the rest?* The answer lies in Dubai's leaders' relentless focus on improving itself, and its refusal to accept "what is" as a substitute for "what could be." "Deliberate Practice," a term coined by psychologist and expertise expert Anders Ericsson, is the idea that to get better you have to practice at it. Expert-level performance is primarily the result of expert-level practice. This isn't to be mistaken with hours simply accumulated while working; rather it's time specifically set aside to practice. For example, a professional golfer gets better by practicing on the range, in the bunker, and on the greens, not just by playing in tournaments.

As I've learned from my CEO coaching business, "being better," and even the desire for it, can be taught. Does that mean that everyone can be the best in the world? No! But if coached properly you can get significantly better. For example, Ahmed (an illustrative name given the confidentiality involved in CEO coaching), was a good leader but what he knew was all he knew. He didn't know what he didn't know. Yet, he assumed he knew everything that he needed to know.

No one had ever taught him to be CEO, or even what CEOs do. So, he just guessed and copied what he thought others did. Sadly, he thought he knew everything about being a CEO, when in reality he knew much less about what he was doing than he ever imagined. Through coaching, though, he was able to expand his field of vision. He began to see his role from a different perspective, and made small adjustments in his leadership style. As a result, his business became the most profitable in its sector.

His limitations had less to do with his innate abilities than simply with what he considered to be an acceptable level of performance. It's always disheartening when I repeatedly hear leaders proclaim they're good at something when in reality they could be much better, like Ahmad could. But in Ahmad's case, as we worked together, he no longer accepted "good enough" as a substitute for the best he could become, and he willingly did the work of going back to "stage one." He started applying the Dubai leadership habits with much success.

Now, he focuses on improving his CEO technique even after he's getting good at it. In other words, he willingly "retreats" from stage three to one—the cognitive stage where he discovers new approaches, becomes more proficient, and constantly seeks feedback on how he can improve.

When you want to be good, shall we say great, how you spend your time practicing becomes far more important than your raw abilities. The secret to improvement is to retain some conscious degree over the process of practicing, not just doing it because it comes naturally now. In leadership-speak, this is "Deliberate Practice."

Emirates Airline deployed deliberate practice shortly after it started buying up A340-500s in the early 2000s. This plane could fly up to seventeen hours, the longest time in the world. One day, president Tim Clark protested in a meeting, "The world thinks no one wants to fly seventeen hours. But they do! It's far more efficient." Previously flights lasted six to seven hours, maybe ten, tops. But while he delighted over the airline's new fleet, Clark focused on how passengers would pass the time. "But what will they do on the plane?" he asked. "Before people would eat some, sleep a little, and maybe do some work." Now, they could do all that twice and still have copious time left over. Clark noted that other carriers flying the A340-500 over long distances but offering the same services as they did on shorter flights.

This simple challenge inspired the Emirates team to create the ICE (Information, Communication, Entertainment) system, which is now Emirates' award-winning in-flight entertainment system. In 2003, Emirates began delivering hundreds of entertainment channels right to passengers' seats, changing not only the passenger experience but the entire industry.

They could have left "good enough" as good enough, but didn't.

Leadership Dubai style embodies a relentless pursuit of improvement, making things better. Henry Ford once said, "Whether you think you can, or you think you can't, you're right." Belief is the basis that you need to instill in your people if you want them to pursue better.

MYSTERY SHOPPERS AND MEASUREMENT

Dubai's use of "mystery shoppers," a form of micro-monitoring, gives us another intriguing example of how the city puts deliberate practice into use. Since the 1940s, companies around the world have relied on "mystery shoppers" to monitor performance. "Mystery shoppers"—that is, "surrogate monitors"—act as customers and provide feedback about their experiences, helping to ensure employees are performing as they should.

Throughout much of Dubai's history, the leader did the lion's share of micro-monitoring. But as Dubai expanded in size, it simply became impossible for the Ruler to be the only "monitor." So, Dubai's Ruling family, along with CEOs of companies and director generals of government entities, turned to surrogate monitors, most of whom reported to the Sheikh. As we discussed before, the interest wasn't to catch someone doing something wrong. It was to elevate the level of performance, and identify where the city could improve.

The usefulness of this practice came into play in August 2004, when Sheikh Mohammed received a frantic call from one of his "mystery shoppers" at the Dubai Airport. It was 1:00 a.m. The news wasn't good.[88]

"Your Highness, the airport is overflowing with people," the mystery shopper said.

"What do you mean?" Sheikh Mohammed asked.

The mystery shopper described the situation: hour-long lines in immigration. People backed up to the planes, barely able to disembark because the airport was full. The situation was so bleak that the mystery shopper suggested Sheikh Mohammed come and have a look himself.

When Sheikh Mohammed arrived, it was immediately clear that the airport was overstretched. Exhausted parents were left trying to comfort their crying kids in immigration lines with crowds of other cranky people. You can only imagine the frustration they felt, having flown long-haul flights in the hopes of getting to their home or hotel right away and putting their kids to bed.

This wasn't acceptable. The end of August was a peak time at the airport; in addition to families returning for the start of the school year, it was also the beginning of conference season. As a convenient connecting point, one that encouraged people to come and succeed, Dubai had established itself as a choice destination for international conferences and exhibitions.

Yet instead of interrupting the already-frightful operation that night, Sheikh Mohammed observed (monitored) what was transpiring and asked the immigration inspectors and on-duty managers to understand the passengers' dilemma. He requested that they speed things up as fast as possible.

Stage three of Fitts and Posner would have Sheikh Mohammed accepting what "was" as "what could be." But that wasn't his style. Obviously there was a dire need to do something. It was time to go back to stage one and discover new ways to be more proficient, and to find new ideas for becoming better.

The next day, Sheikh Mohammed called a meeting with airport leaders. His aim wasn't to berate them, nor did he want to spend undue time talking about what went wrong. His focus was on what he really wanted—the airport to be better in the future. He invited top customs and immigration officials, as well as airline representatives, the airport administration, and the airport's customer care team. Terminal three, which would become the second-largest building in the world (measured by floor space) and the world's largest airport terminal, with a capacity of forty-three million passengers, was still under construction. It would take several more years to become operational.

"We need interim solutions to get things moving," Sheikh Mohammed said. "The airport is our vital lifeline to the world and the place that shapes the first impression of Dubai." Knowing that, he asked each attendee: "How can the airport serve passengers better?" It was a recurring question in the Ruler's quest to keep everyone focused.

After brainstorming together for a few hours, leaders took immediate action. Instantly, Dubai Airport increased capacity by adding new immigration desks. Probably the biggest improvement came through the E-Gate system, which enabled passengers to bypass standard passport control with a flash of a card and the press of a thumb. Over the next decade, as the pursuit of getting better continued—and airport traffic more than tripled—the average immigration time *decreased* to just twenty seconds. Queuing up at passport control could soon be a thing of the past.

In addition to mystery shoppers, another tool Dubai uses to become better is measurement. In the case of Dubai Airport, officials measured passenger transit times—the number of minutes between landing and the time a person passes through the immigration counters. This gave officials clear metrics, and helped them set targets, to make the flow faster. In turn this reduced the pressure on the airport.

Generally speaking if you're in the "fold" of Sheikh Mohammed's oversight, there are expected results you must deliver on: no excuses are accepted. Performance, and usually ahead of schedule—is the only thing tolerated.

Frankly, if you're not up for the challenge to continually perform, you should have jitters if you're looking at working under Sheikh Mohammed. During an announcement about the "Smart Government" program, which would optimize the government's online services, Sheikh Mohammed said, "He who cannot keep up with the changes will not achieve the developments. Therefore, we will hold a farewell party (after two years) for one of your brothers or one who is dear to you, because he failed to keep up with the developments. Actually we are launching the smart government, and I hope there will be no one from (among) you who lagged behind in this field."[89]

When I think about measuring performance, words from my dad again ring in my ear: "Measure, remeasure, and measure again." While he was speaking of cutting a piece of wood, this also proves true when it comes to getting better. Constant measuring keeps you posted on what matters most, while at the same time revealing weaker areas where you can improve.

SET THE MARK

Starting in 1994, Sheikh Mohammed launched the Dubai Quality Awards as a means of improving the standards of businesses operating in Dubai, thus boosting external and internal trade. Companies compete against one another, showcasing their commitment to quality in all areas of their business. Even the measurement of quality has been put to the test to continually improve, as Dubai introduced similar programs to the Dubai Quality Awards. The pursuit of excellence is continuous and does not stop at any limits.

To succeed in these competitions—and in any arena in business—you have to embrace the idea that things can always get better. You have limitless opportunities to improve, and you must set the standard. Given companies' desire to win a Dubai Quality Award, Sheikh Mohammed has effectively embedded across the city the non-acceptance of the status quo. He is keeping people who don't even work for him in stage one. The Dubai Quality Awards guidelines and subsequent feedback report make leaders conscious of the work they're doing, and forces them to discover new ways to operate more proficiently. By setting the standard, you can give your company a maniacal focus on becoming the best.

A few years back, I heard Microsoft confess that the government of Dubai was pushing them to create solutions that were significant improvements on what others were doing. When first launching e-government, Microsoft made the easy mistake of sharing with the Dubai government what others around the world were doing, thinking they would accept these as best practices. But the government didn't want to copy what others were doing and then get the same results. They pushed Microsoft to come up with technology solutions that were better than what Microsoft had already proposed to them. And, they did! The government of Dubai became the first Arab state to offer e-government.

Microsoft was surprised that Dubai was pushing them for more, since it was usually the software giant pushing governments forward. Dubai's focus on continuous improvement was vastly different from the mentality of most of Microsoft's governmental clients, who insisted on copying "best practices."

Another example, this time from the aviation industry, shows how Dubai pushes their partners to "be better" too. GE Aviation is one of the world's top aircraft engine suppliers, providing engines for the majority of commercial aircraft, including Emirates Airline. Several years ago, Emirates Airline turned to GE Aviation asking for an unheard-of solution. At the time it was common for an engine to be able to fly forty-five hundred to five thousand hours per year. Emirates wanted more! They wanted six thousand hours per year without compromising quality or creating a safety concern. And that is what was delivered.

No matter who you are—a government department

head, the CEO of Microsoft, or an engineer at GE Aviation—when doing business in Dubai you are challenged to set the mark. This means improving to the level where others will copy you and try to perform against you. "Where is the progress in keeping pace with the competition?" Sheikh Mohammed challenged a group of ministers when he was still Crown Prince. The ministers didn't believe it was necessary to keep developing. ". . . Do not fool yourselves into believing that we are moving forward when we are only keeping up with general trends, while the real opportunities slip away."[90] Dubai pushes you to the max!

If you lag behind in Dubai, or anywhere else for that matter, you become irrelevant in a heartbeat. If you want to be taken seriously as a leader you must stay in stage one, continually working to get better. Remember, too, that there comes a time when it isn't enough to get better by bringing outside ideas in. You have to become the engine of innovation rather than relying on an imitation or a "fast follower" strategy.

For a long time in Dubai, leaders looked outside the country for "better" ideas. During his time as Ruler, Sheikh Rashid would frequently travel outside the country—during which, he often willingly went off the beaten path. Without the Internet, or another high-tech means of acquiring information, realistically, where else would he get his "big" ideas besides traveling abroad? On official visits he'd often veer off from the official itinerary, turning up at Fun Fairs or touring the London Underground. He was fascinated with what he experienced. His openness to outside ideas enlarged his own thoughts as to how much better Dubai could be.

Sheikh Rashid wasn't the only one who was looking outside of Dubai. As we'll discuss in the next chapter, starting in the mid-1970s students were sent all around the world to receive their educations. And business leaders such as Mohammad Alabbar (Singapore), Majid Al Futtaim (Japan), and others spent time outside of the UAE, learning and then importing and integrating what they learned into Dubai.

In 2008, Nabil Al-Yousuf, then adviser to Sheikh Mohammed, proudly proclaimed in a *New York Times* article, "Part of our mission in Dubai is to bring the best practices from outside."[91] But that's not "good enough" for Dubai anymore. Today, leaders push global firms to do what has never been before. They influence their vendors to do what people say cannot be done. Leading Dubai style doesn't ask you to do what you are able: it asks you to do the seemingly impossible.

In recent months, Sheikh Mohammed has sent a clear, consistent message that it's time for Dubai to be the place where others come for ideas—not the other way around. On his LinkedIn page in February 2015, he wrote, "Innovation in government isn't an intellectual luxury, a topic to be confined to seminars and panel discussions, or a matter only of administrative reforms. It is the recipe for human survival and development, the fuel for constant progress, and the blueprint for a nation's rise."[92]

Sheikh Mohammed doesn't accept excuses. "I'll do it tomorrow" are words he cautions anyone against ever saying. In Dubai there's no time to sit around and talk about what you'll do. Great honor comes with delivery, in actually making Dubai the best. If you say you're going to do something, you create the expectation that you'll carry through with it. "If we're able to do it today to strengthen our economy today, then it should be done today," he said at a government summit in 2013.[93]

In a 2002 meeting with government leaders from around the world, Sheikh Mohammed advised, "If we want a productive administration, our objectives must be realistic, not based on dreams and good intentions. These objectives must be developed into action plans. We also need to have the right people and review their progress."[94] What he really said was, "Do it!" Once Sheikh Mohammed gives the green light to a project, he expects that it will be done—and that's that.

"It's good enough!" are words you'll never hear in Dubai. Here, best-practice thinking is most valuable when you're creating the best practice, not copying it. Stay in stage one so you never settle for being simply "good enough." Constantly pursue getting better. Always be searching for faster and better ways.

TWELVE

Who's after Me?

——Leadership Habit——
LEAD TODAY FOR TOMORROW'S FUTURE

Ever since its inception in 1971, the UAE has been focused on—dare I say obsessed with—developing leaders from within. You could also say it's had no choice.

On the country's Unification Day on December 2, 1971, a joyful, celebratory mood permeated the air in Abu Dhabi, with the country's prominent families hosting special lunches and dinners. But brand-new president Sheikh Zayed focused on the tasks that lay ahead: How, he had to have wondered, would the UAE handle its own affairs with no diplomatic service in place? The British had taken care of all that before. Now that they were gone, who would replace them? The cabinet was to assume power without any formal government apparatus, established ministries, or government buildings, and no civil servants and no history of such national structures. It was a blank slate.[95]

The president decided to put out word—an urgent request, largely passed by word of mouth—for all BA graduates from Dubai and the Northern Emirates to attend a meeting regarding positions in the Diplomatic Service. Mirza Al Sayegh, who now works in the office of Sheikh Hamdan bin Rashid and is a board member of Emirates National Oil Company Ltd. (ENOC), was on his way to his first day of work with Dubai Petroleum Company when he heard the message. He decided to take a detour. "I didn't know what job or what salary we were being offered," he told me as we sipped tea in his stately office in Jebel Ali. "It was a risk! But I went out of duty."[96]

Twenty-five men showed up: Yes, only twenty-five people had a bachelor's degree or higher (excluding doctors) in Dubai in 1971!

Immediately, the government began sending students around the world to get their university education. People are the base of any civilization, and the UAE rightfully chose to use its resources—namely, a young population—to drive development. Maximizing the youthful population would give the UAE the demographic dividend, which is when a disproportionate percentage of a country's population is comprised of young working-age, and result in the national economy being positively affected.

Every year, more and more students scattered across campuses around the world to learn from the best professors and then come back to help build up their country. By the 1980s Dubai was getting a solid return on its investment in education. Talented and ambitious Emiratis were welcomed back with open arms. The best ones were spotted, groomed, and placed in leadership positions. They were then watched to see if they could perform; if they did, they were given greater responsibilities.

Perhaps unbeknownst to Sheikh Zayed, he was also being closely observed—by his mentee, Sheikh Mohammed. "I learned a lot from him," says Sheikh Mohammed, then minister of defense and head of Dubai Police, of those thrilling early days with his role model. "He would ask me questions and involve me in discussions. I would see how he dealt with other leaders and what he did. Sheikh Zayed was the best leader! I learned much more from him, more than even from school. He advised me [on] how to face challenges, and [how to] meet people and politicians."[97]

SUCCESSION THINKING

As we've seen throughout these pages, the Rulers have made it a point to consciously consider and prepare their successors—that is, to ask, "Who's after me?" Thinking about tomorrow, today isn't just a strategy for developing a country's physical infrastructure. Thinking about tomorrow also includes carefully preparing who will lead next. Sheikh Maktoum bin Hasher's father and grandfather, for example, instilled in him the need to promote Dubai's trade base—a habit he imparted to his son, Sheikh Saeed. And Sheikh Rashid deliberately raised his boys to be future leaders of Dubai, just as Sheikh Mohammed is doing with his. Since its founding, leading Dubai style is about preparing leaders for tomorrow, today.

As I know from my work with my clients, and also from living in the region for so long, many family businesses struggle with succession thinking, wondering how to prepare their children to take over. Yet right in front of their eyes is a model they can follow. Since the mid-1800s Dubai has skillfully passed the leadership baton to six successive generations and eleven different leaders.

One of the secrets of the Ruling family's success is exposing young leaders to future challenges before they have the responsibility or authority to fix them. Sheikh Rashid welcomed his boys into his majlis and encouraged them to work alongside him in his office. Even in their early teens, these "boys" were experienced and mature leaders within the administration. Sheikh Rashid allowed his sons to see exactly what he was doing and how he was doing it, thus shaping them for when they themselves would have positions of authority. By giving early exposure, you effectively fast-track people's learning and minimize the time it takes to reach optimal leadership performance.

Sheikh Rashid also introduced his sons to the sport of hunting at an early age, as an overall strategic part of their development. He did this partly because it was his ideal relaxation and respite from the mental intensity of building a city, and more so to teach them to be keen thinkers—to concentrate, use discipline, and exercise care. Before they became full-fledged hunters, they were required to watch and gain knowledge from other hunters, which shaped them to be sharp observers of their surroundings and others' actions. This must have seeped in more than the actual skills of the sport, as much of their leadership behavior was based on the lessons they learned in those early days.

As we've seen all throughout this book, the "Rashid Leadership Academy," while lacking "professors" and a formal curriculum, was every bit as effective as a real "school" in developing leadership abilities. Today, Sheikh Mohammed has the same "succession" thinking as did his father and in a very similar way raises his sons to rule Dubai. I'm still intrigued by the conversations that must have happened around their dinner table. Did father and sons dream together about hosting EXPO 2020? Do they discuss Dubai becoming number one? Do they openly commit to creating an environment where others could succeed?

KEEP AN EYE ON HIM

Along with preparing successors, Dubai's leaders make it a point to consistently be on the lookout for rising talent within the ranks—the art of "spotting" and "grooming," as I mentioned earlier.

One of the most successful stories of Dubai-style "spotting" comes from Mohammed Al Gergawi, now minister of cabinet affairs. In his late twenties, Gergawi held a mid-level job in the Department of Economic Development as the director of business registration. During his first week on the job, an old man walked into Gergawi's office, seemingly lost. When they began speaking, Gergawi realized that this man was a good friend of his late father, Abdulla.[98]

"Remember that the chair you are sitting on is like a barber's chair," the man told him.

"What do you mean a 'barber's chair'?" Gergawi asked, confused.

The man explained that when you go the barber, you never sit on the chair for long—somebody else always comes along. It's a temporary seat.

"So while you're sitting on that chair, try to be good to people and help people as much as possible," the man said. "You shouldn't let any job go to your head. This is a barber's chair and you don't need to have a desk."

This simple bit of advice sobered Gergawi and stuck with him. After the man left, he removed his desk and started to operate without one. Getting rid of the desk meant that Gergawi started working outside his office, among the people. Many elderly Emiratis had never learned to read or write, so he helped them fill out the proper forms and escorted them to the proper counter when they were finished. Anyone who arrived looking confused, he helped.

But he was a director! He didn't need to do this. . . .

Unbeknownst to Gergawi, one of the elderly gentlemen he helped with a little paperwork was one of Sheikh Mohammed's mystery shoppers. After the shopper submitted a report highlighting Gergawi's exemplary behavior, Sheikh Mohammed instructed him to keep an eye on the young Gergawi. Gergawi had been spotted! Now he was watched to see how he performed. Sheikh Mohammed's people learned that under his leadership the department got better—it became more efficient, and customer satisfaction rose.

A few years later, Gergawi was offered a job in the private sector, which would nearly triple his salary. For Gergawi, this meant a whole lot. He had grown up in a modest home, and had to cope, at just twelve years of age, with his beloved father's untimely death. Money had always been tight in his household.

A few days after receiving the offer, Gergawi submitted his resignation to take the higher-paying job. When Sheikh Mohammed got the news, he decided to make a better offer and promote him to the number two job, which would make Gergawi the deputy director of the Dubai Department of Economic Development. Incidentally Gergawi's boss became Mohammed Alabbar, and the two of them went on to become two of the most significant leaders in the modern chapter of Dubai's leadership story.

When Gergawi shared this great news with his mother, with whom he is very close, she encouraged, actually demanded, that he go and thank Sheikh Mohammed for the promotion in person at his majlis. Nervous, he headed to Za'abeel Palace.

Well over a hundred people were attending, which made Gergawi even more hesitant and scared. Finally he walked over to thank Sheikh Mohammed, nervously saying, "Your Highness, you don't know me. My name is Mohammed Al Gergawi. You promoted me two months ago. I'm just here to say thank you very much. With God's help, I can live up to your expectations. I hope I can deliver."

As Gergawi stood to walk away, Sheikh Mohammed pulled at his hand to make him sit back down. The majlis became very quiet.

"Mohammed, I know you well actually, and I've been following you for the past four or five years. I know what you do—and this is the beginning for you, actually." The message for everyone was loud and clear: spot leadership talent and grow it. You are responsible for building tomorrow's leaders, today.

Knowing that Dubai's future success is dependent on the quality of its leaders, Sheikh Mohammed has built an environment where outstanding leaders are constantly sought after and verified. Before promoting somebody, leaders put that person to the test. Though they believe their prospects are able, leaders want to be certain they'll continue to perform.

Looking deep into your business or organization to spot future leaders and keeping your eye on them is exactly what you should be doing. It's a pity that most companies only pay lip service to identifying future leaders, saying, "Yes, it is important that we identify our future leaders." And then these hollow words are repeated year after year with no action. Not in Dubai—day after day, leaders are identified and observed for their potential in fulfilling future positions.

In Gergawi's case, Sheikh Mohammed came through on his promise. Today, along with being minister of cabinet affairs, Gergawi is leading the development of the UAE Federal Government Strategy. He is also the chairman of the Sheikh Mohammed bin Rashid Al Maktoum Executive Office and Foundation, as well as the chairman of Dubai Holding, an investment holding company composed of Jumeirah Hotels, TECOM, Dubai Properties, and several other valuable assets.

GROW THEM, TOO

While Sheikh Mohammed clearly has an eye for spotting talent, he also *grows* people to become future leaders. The Dubai Government Excellence Programme (DGEP), established in September 1997, is one of those ways.

The DGEP focuses specifically on developing the eighty thousand governmental employees in the emirate. It is the first integrated program for governmental excellence in the world. Through continual learning, training, and monitoring, Dubai experiences quantum-leap performance improvement year after year. In a survey conducted by the British Standards Institution (BSI), over 89 percent of DGEP participants stated that the program helped government entities achieve the vision of Sheikh Mohammed. And a similar percentage attributed their achievement of higher levels of excellence, on par with international norms, to the program.[99]

The DGEP is merely one example of Dubai's numerous and notable "employee development" programs. Others include the Mohammed bin Rashid Leadership Programs and the Dubai School of Government programs, to name but a couple. Spots in these programs are highly coveted, and participants who attend wear a badge of honor. While these programs are important, what is more so is that Dubai makes leaders' growth a priority.

"I keep track of each step of the training program and I am happy with its development," says Sheikh Mohammed. "[Young people] guarantee that development will continue and sustainability will prevail. We are preparing them for this future by developing them to promote innovation, creativity, and entrepreneurship."[100]

Personally, Dubai's emphasis on building capable leaders and the talk of it "around town" is among the highest enthusiasm I've ever experienced in both the public and private sectors. In the past two and half decades of studying top leaders in various companies and countries, I've never seen anything close to this level of conviction. The constant emphasis on growing leaders and the commitment to make programs better and better amazes me. This is the bedrock, the backbone, of Dubai's ability to pass on leadership habits to the next generation.

However, something I've learned from years of working with businesses and governments is that this is also the most neglected leadership habit for many organizations. Oftentimes, this habit is skipped entirely, because of the time and cost involved. It's easy to assume you can get around to this later, under the guise that it isn't mission critical. Warning:

if you skip this habit, you are setting yourself up for certain failure.

It *is* mission critical. Everything rises and falls on leadership. Your success will be achieved or limited by how good your leaders are. Developing people is an obsession you should have. You should be building the leadership prowess of your city or company, always thinking a decade or more into the future. Your investment today will quickly be realized, as it was in Dubai.

Only a few short decades ago, Dubai had only twenty-five bachelor's degree holders. Today Dubai is home to countless degree-holders, many of whom are among the leading thinkers in the world. These thinkers include Dr. Maryam Matar, founder of the UAE Genetic Disease Association and former director general of the Community Development Authority. A certified family physician and now completing her PhD research at Yamaguchi University in Japan, she was the first Emirati woman to bear the title of Undersecretary to the Minister of Health. Now, she's leading the UAE to be free of Thalassemia, one of the UAE's most common blood diseases.

Matar and thousands of other native Emiratis are the direct product of the UAE's investment in education. Today, 95 percent of female Emirati high school graduates pursue further education at tertiary-level institutions (compared with 80 percent of males).[101] This is a big change in just a few decades, a change that has only come about by a constant focus on capability development. Sheikh Zayed wasn't satisfied with only a handful of degree holders; he wanted more, to invest in building capability for the future.

Again, I'd like to emphasize: if you copy everything in this book and skip this chapter, you *will* fail for the simple reason that achieving remarkable success requires breadth and depth of leadership. It's simply not possible to do this by yourself; the task is too big for you alone. You need to build your leadership capability, today, so you have a cadre of Dubai-style leaders to take over, tomorrow.

In Dubai, this leadership habit comes first. Without the best—not average—leaders, we wouldn't have Dubai. Tomorrow's leaders are today's responsibility. With a clear eye on the future, build who will lead tomorrow, today. Think ten years or more into the future. If you put this habit off until tomorrow, you'll compromise the whole leadership model outlined in this book.

CONCLUSION

"The word impossible isn't in the leader's dictionary."
—*Sheikh Mohammed bin Rashid Al Maktoum*

A couple of decades ago, most people had never heard of Dubai. Now, "Where's Dubai?" has been replaced by "Destination Dubai." Wherever I travel in the world, I hear, "Oh, you live in Dubai!" proclaimed with incredible enthusiasm—and maybe more than a little envy.

"How lucky you are to live where things are happening," people wistfully say. People who visit go home and dream about it, wishing they could have Dubai where they live. People who work in Dubai and then return to their home countries try and export the experience. "Why can't we be the same?" they ask. "Why can't we benefit from Dubai's experience and have leadership like that?" To many, Dubai is the modern-day land of milk and honey—a promise of success.

Businesses and foreign governments also want what Dubai represents—they want the "Dubai effect." And they should! Around the world, when countries are facing presidential elections or a change in leadership, "Give us Mohammed bin Rashid" campaigns regularly pop up on Facebook.

I wrote this book because of my obsession with helping leaders grow. But as we all know, growth can be challenging. After reading this book you might, frankly, find yourself a little shaken up. Recently, after giving a speech to a group of

Harvard Business School alumni about my findings, I was asked, "Are you saying the models we're all using, even what we were taught in business school, are suboptimal?" The concerned look in the executives' eyes spoke volumes.

I stood in the boardroom on the fourteenth floor of the Gate building in Dubai International Financial Centre, one of Dubai's most visually stunning Free Zones. Floor-to-ceiling windows framed a picture-perfect view of the Burj Khalifa and Downtown Dubai. I took a dramatic pause, looking toward the window to draw everyone's attention to it.

"Yes!" I proclaimed. I told them that Dubai-style leadership achieves results that, at the government level, are unheard of and, in a corporate setting, are rare. In my work, where I consult with CEOs and government leaders, I continually challenge my clients to break from the existing leadership approaches so they can embrace the habits from this book.

While researching for *Leadership Dubai Style*, I kept asking myself, "Can others do this? Can governments and business leaders copy Dubai's leadership style?" Yes! You can absolutely emulate it. The twelve leadership habits presented here are transferable to any industry or organization, large or small, private or public. Whether you are based in or outside of Dubai, these habits are for you. If you're interested in learning even more, the "Habits for Growing Against the Odds" leadership program brings each of these leadership habits to life, and helps organizations achieve what Dubai has. (For more information on this program, visit: www.tommyweir.com.)

Now, before I bid you on your way to achieving remarkable success, I wanted to take a few minutes and recap how to apply these habits.

First, you need to determine your purpose. You must

complete this step, as this purpose will form the nucleus of your success and will be the basis for your leadership. Ask yourself: What do you want to achieve? Next—be hungry with ambition. You have to be starved in order to lead Dubai style. Remember that even after the discovery of oil, leaders worked harder than ever in reinvesting their newfound wealth in the original purpose—to be a notable hub where others could succeed.

Once you've committed to your strategy, give people space to deliver—create an environment in which others can succeed. "Micro-monitor but don't micromanage" is the operative phrase here. If anyone gets off track, speak up and help that person get back on course and become "better." Cultivate loyalty by conducting your own version of a "majlis," where you consult to listen and don't fall into the consensus trap. If a crisis hits, don't panic! And most importantly, don't ever be a jerk. I know these habits require you to be decisive, even autocratic, but that doesn't mean you should ever disrespect people or take a power trip—if you do, stop!

Also, always look toward the future: this is the nexus of what this model is about.

Remember, these habits are meant to be integrated together: if you skip any one of them, or practice any in isolation, you risk compromising the whole model, and could have a formula for disaster on your hands.

I realize these habits may be a bit challenging to implement. They might directly contradict what you have probably been taught about leadership, in possibly expensive courses and schools. I don't know what to say about that, other than getting different results requires forming different habits.

A word about habit building: by following the principles

in this book, you'll probably be forming and breaking habits at the same time. I know how hard changing habits can be, so here's a good way to start: make what you're going to do conscious by writing it down. Putting what you want to achieve in writing improves the odds of your doing it. You can improve your odds even more so by involving somebody to keep you accountable—perhaps a coach or another stakeholder who wants to see you succeed. This simple habit-building formula centers on reminders (to keep you focused on what you should do), routine (the actions you take), and rewards—in other words, what you gain from these leadership habits.

Sheikh Mohammed once said, "In life there are two paths—one creates success and the other creates a loser. During my lifetime I've met many people with negative energy who make excuses and alibis. To a sunny day they will say, 'No, it is cloudy or foggy,' without even opening the curtains to have a peek."[102]

Some people want to look at Dubai and find its flaws. Given the media's tendency to criticize Dubai—and, let's be fair, not all of Dubai's practices always lend themselves to praise—I was very mindful of the fact that I'd probably be asked for criticisms. But focusing on Dubai's flaws is a waste of time. From a theoretical perspective, the areas that you may want to poke a finger at may just be what led to Dubai's desired outcome. So, learn from Dubai's successes instead. As Sheikh Mohammed says, "Why should you think about failure, when you can think about success?"[103]

Apply the lessons from this book and boldly lead Dubai style. Don't worry about it being different or even hard. If you want similar results, start where you are with what you have. Lead! Don't give up!

If at any point along the way you want support, I can be reached either through my website, listed earlier, or directly via tsw@tommyweir.com. If you'd like me to come speak to your organization about the leadership habits that achieve remarkable success, please contact the London Speaker Bureau.

I wish you the best of luck in building new, lasting leadership habits!

—Dr. Tommy Weir, October 2015

ABOUT THE RESEARCH

After three years of solid research, I finally felt ready to share my conclusions in this book. My quest began with an exhaustive literature review about Dubai. I sifted through doctoral dissertations, books about Dubai's history, and popular writings on the city. The topics of these writings ranged from architectural insights, sports, and economics to social issues, including people's personal experiences living in Dubai. I even delved into popular novels to get an insight into what leaders were doing.

I discovered that while there's been a lot written about Dubai, there aren't any works that take a look at the emirate from a leadership or management point of view. Previous works either focused on Dubai's history, which is very limited in printed word due to the fact that Dubai is primarily an oral culture, or Dubai's modernity, focusing only on the last decade or two. Along with these were pieces critiquing Dubai's successes, commenting on what Dubai "should have done."

I backed this literature review with two hundred "qualitative" interviews with people who had a front-row seat to the developments in Dubai. The interviewees were split into three groupings: Emiratis (people from the UAE) who contributed to the growth of the city (you could say they were "pillars of growth"), Emiratis who saw how the leaders led but who weren't in the inner circle, and expatriates who built companies in Dubai, both privately and state-owned enterprises.

In the qualitative research I paid particular attention to:
Recurrence. Was the habit practiced by multiple leaders or was it a one-off instance? Was it passed from one generation to the next?
Reference. Given that the Gulf is a historically oral culture, and that there are gaps in time and variation of facts based on who shared the information, it was imperative to consider the quality of the information and the proximity/relationship of the source to the insights they shared. To determine their reliability, I considered the integrity of any related anecdotes shared and the quality of the balance of the interview. Basically, I was answering, "Does he know what he is saying? Can his information be relied on or is it merely an opinion?"

Given that this was the first comprehensive study of Dubai's leadership practices, I found it necessary to build upon my broader work on Arab leadership and more importantly, leadership in general. It was also necessary to explore other founder/leaders in founder-based organizations around the world such as Red Bull, Ford, Wal-Mart, Apple, and Ralph Lauren to sense-check the insights that emerged.

After collecting all the information, I conducted an analysis to estimate the relationship between the leadership insights (independent variables) and Dubai's sustained results measured by Dubai's growth (dependent variable). The aim of the research was to answer what caused Dubai's success from a leadership point of view. The result of the analysis is the twelve habits in this book, which in turn form "The Habits of Remarkable Success" model.

END NOTES

1 This is the newer translation of Sheikh Mohammed bin Rashid Al Maktoum's poem "A Challenge," which was originally published (English version) in *40 Poems from the Desert* (Dubai: Motivate Publishing, 2011).

Introduction

2 Shakir Husain, "The Pillars of Society: Farid Mohammad Ahmad," *Gulf News*, September 30, 2008.

3 Yuwa Hedrick-Wong and Desmond Choong, "2014 Global Destination Cities Index," *MasterCard Worldwide Insights*, 2014, 3.

4 CBRE News, "Dubai Retains Second Position for International Retailer Representation for Fourth Consecutive Year," CBRE, the world's largest real estate investment manager, May 18, 2015.

5 Dubai Tourism Press Release, "Dubai Welcomes 13.2m International Visitors in 2014," May 3, 2015.

6 The UAE (United Arab Emirates) is a country composed of seven emirates.

7 The Ruler is the principle Sheikh responsible for his whole population and geography. Similar to a monarch, he is the highest authority and sovereign head. The primary difference, as we will see later, is that the selection process comes from the people's allegiance and loyalty.

The Crown Prince is the heir apparent to become the next Ruler.

Chapter One

8 The Bani Yas were one of the most prestigious and highly regarded tribes of Southern Arabia. They ruled the land we now know as the Empty Quarter—the largest sand desert in the world, including

the ancient cities of Liwa, Al Ain, and Abu Dhabi. Partly because of their numerical superiority, but mainly because of their military prowess and proven loyalty to allies, many other tribes sought to join the Bani Yas for protection and security.

The two primary branches of the Bani Yas tribe (there were about twenty in total) were the Al Falahi, ancestors of the modern-day Ruling family of Abu Dhabi, the Al Nahyans, and the Al Bu Falasah, ancestors of many of Dubai's Al Maktoums.

9 In an oral culture, events pass verbally from one generation to the next and from one family to the other by telling stories. These stories are often accompanied by embellishments or omissions to highlight what is important to the storyteller.

10 Raja Trad, conversation with the author, February 18, 2014.

11 2012 International Council of Shopping Centres (ICSC) research report.

12 Throughout *Leadership Dubai Style*, you'll regularly see the word "majlis," which literally means "a place of sitting." It is a meeting room in a home where guests are hosted (many homes have a separate majlis for the men and women). Practically speaking it is the gathering place where leaders and the people of the community come together to discuss their affairs.

In an official sense—and in the primary usage in this book—the majlis is the place where government leaders and leading businessmen discuss what is taking place in the greater community. Later on, we'll discuss the role of the majlis as one of the twelve leadership habits.

13 In the evenings, actually late nights, it is common for leaders to open their homes to receive and entertain guests. Some, like Mr. Majid, offer a full meal. The Ramadan majlis deepens the bonds among

the members of the family, friends, relatives, and even strangers, who are welcome to visit.

14 "His Highness Sheikh Mohammed bin Rashid Al Maktoum: Early Life," Sheikh Mohammed's official website, accessed July 15, 2015.

15 Ibid.

Chapter Two

16 Ram Charan, Stephen Drotter, and James Noel. *The Leadership Pipeline: How to Build the Leadership Powered Company* (San Francisco: Jossey-Bass, 2001).

17 As you'll see in the coming chapters, this was the beginning of the modern era of Dubai's development, when the physical infrastructure for future growth was built (expanded port and airport, better road network, etc.). During this time, the focus expanded to Dubai becoming a destination, thus fueling the investment in retail, tourism, and freehold property.

18 Graeme Wilson, *Rashid's Legacy* (London: Media Prima, 2006), 188.

19 Osman Sultan, conversation with the author, February 19, 2014.

20 "Women in the UAE," Sheikh Mohammed's official website, accessed August 1, 2015.

21 Mohammed bin Rashid Al Maktoum, *Flashes of Thought* (Dubai: Motivate Publishing, 2013), 44.

22 WAM, "UAE Ranks First in World for Respecting Women," *Gulf News*, April 27, 2014.

23 Nick Webster, "Women of the UAE: Mariana Garcia Garza," *The National*, May 17, 2015.

Chapter Three

24 Alexander Cornwell, "Dubai World Central Airport Opens to

Passengers," *Gulf News*, October 26, 2013.

25 Amina Al Rustamani, conversation with the author, January 13, 2015.

26 "Interview: Zayan Ghandour," Visit Dubai website, accessed August 1, 2015, http://www.visitdubai.com/en/articles/interview-zayan-ghandour

Chapter Four

27 Ahmed Hassan Al Shaikh, conversation with the author, April 25, 2013.

28 This poem is credited to several different sources, potentially originating in the *Economist* magazine in 1985 in an article titled "Lions or Gazelles?" where the words were credited to a securities analyst named Dan Montano.

29 Mohammed bin Rashid Al Maktoum, *My Vision* (Dubai: Motivate Publishing, 2012), 12.

30 Graeme Wilson, *Rashid's Legacy* (London: Media Prima, 2006), 365.

31 Mohammed bin Rashid Al Maktoum, remarks at the World Economic Forum, Jordan, May 16, 2004.

32 Sheikh Rashid knew that his sons would one day take over the leadership of Dubai, just as he had in the same tradition of his father, grandfather, and great-grandfather. There was no doubt in his mind that early on they would be expected to handle some of the affairs of the city—finances, defense, safety, and relations with the other emirates, to name a few. I wonder if he had a premonition in the 1950s that just a decade later his boys would be an integral part of forming the United Arab Emirates.

33 Mirza Al Sayegh, conversation with the author, February 6, 2015.

34 Linda Mahoney, conversation with the author, January 6, 2015.

35 Mohammed bin Rashid Al Maktoum, question-and-answer ses-

sion at the first "UAE Government Summit," February 11, 2013.

36 Sultan Bin Sulayem, conversation with the author, November 25, 2008.

37 Dubai Internet City is now home to 1,400 companies, including Fortune 500-listed companies and multinationals such as Facebook, Google, IBM, Mastercard, Microsoft, and LinkedIn. Dubai Media City is now the Middle East and North Africa (MENA) region's largest hub dedicated to the media industry, and a thriving business community with 1,500 leading international and regional media brands, including global giants CNN and Thomson Reuters.

38 Shane McGinley, "Interview: DIFC Courts Chief Mark Beer," *Arabian Business*, November 2, 2013.

39 If you're curious about what could be perceived as a discrepancy between the thirteen million tourists and the number of visitors to Dubai's malls and the Dubai Shopping Festival, there is a logical explanation. The difference is twofold, as the latter accounts for: 1) tourists, residents, and even residents and tourists who came from another emirate, and 2) multiple visits. For example, if a tourist comes to Dubai for a four-day trip, that counts as one tourist. Yet, she may visit Dubai Mall three different times, creating three visits to Dubai Mall as well as probably visiting Mall of the Emirates and other malls; thus the astounding number of visits to the malls each year.

40 Mohammed bin Rashid Al Maktoum, question-and-answer session at the first "UAE Government Summit," February 11, 2013.

41 Mohamed Alabbar, interview by Steve Harvey, *Emirates World Interviews*, January 2015.

Chapter Five

42 Maurice Flanagan, conversation with the author, January 20, 2015.

43 Malcolm Wall Morris, conversation with the author, April 30, 2013.

44 Paul Griffiths, conversation with the author, July 10, 2014.

Chapter Six

45 Generation Research is an independent Swedish research firm that produces the Best & Most—an important everyday tool for industry professionals. The wealth of data available to Generation has led to the establishment of Best & Most as the principal work of reference for the worldwide duty free and travel retail business.

46 This is the fourth time that DDF has been named the largest retail operation, ahead of Seoul Incheon, Singapore Changi, and London Heathrow airport. The Dubai-based airport retailer was previously named the largest in 2008, 2009, and 2010.

47 Interview with Mohammed bin Rashid Al Maktoum, *60 Minutes*, October 14, 2007.

48 WAM Press Release, "Mohammed Bin Rashid Launches Mall of the World, a Temperature-Controlled Pedestrian City in Dubai," July 5, 2014.

49 Ahmed bin Butti, conversation with the author, December 19, 2012.

50 While Sheikh Rashid officially became the Ruler of Dubai in 1958, given his vision, enthusiasm, and energy, he took a leading role in the development of Dubai starting in the 1930s. His father, Sheikh Saeed, gladly welcomed and encouraged Sheikh Rashid's leadership.

51 Graeme Wilson, *Rashid's Legacy* (London: Media Prima, 2006), 93.

52 Tim Clark, speech for Bureau International des Expositions, October 22, 2013.

53 His Highness Sheikh Mohammed Twitter page, https://twitter.com/HHSHKMOHD, May 23, 2015.

54 "The Airport of the Future," Dubai Airport's 2050 Plan.

55 Ahmad Hassan Al Shaikh, "Is Dubai's Competitive Advantage Sustainable? A Study of Strategic Planning in Dubai 1996 to 2010." PhD diss., Coventry University, 2012.

56 Department of Economic Development, Government of Dubai. "Into the 21st Century: A Strategic Plan to Build a Fully Diversified and Prosperous Economy," 1996.

57 Department of Economic Development, Government of Dubai. "New Dubai in a New Economy: Dubai Strategic Development Plan (2003–2007)," 2003.

58 The Executive Office, Government of Dubai. "Highlights Dubai Strategic Plan (2007–2015)," February 2007.

59 General Secretariat of the Executive Council, Government of Dubai. "Dubai Plan 2021," 2014.

60 Ibid., p. 7.

61 Mohammed bin Rashid Al Maktoum, *Flashes of Thought* (Dubai: Motivate Publishing, 2013), 54–55.

Chapter Seven

62 Gerald Lawless, conversation with the author, March 25, 2014.

63 Stephen Bradley and Pankaj Ghemawat, "Wal*Mart Stores, Inc.," HBS No. 9-794-024 (Boston: Harvard Business School Publishing, 2002), 1.

64 Ibid., 4.

65 Ahmed Bahrozyan, conversation with the author, April 26, 2015.

66 WAM Press Release, "Mohammed Bin Rashid Views Results of Transition to M-Government," May 23, 2015.

67 Conversation with the author, December 19, 2012.

68 "His Highness Sheikh Mohammed bin Rashid Al Maktoum: Early Life," Sheikh Mohammed's official website, accessed August 1, 2015.

Chapter Eight

69 The president is the head of state of the UAE. Officially he is elected every five years by the Federal Supreme Council, but because the Ruler of Abu Dhabi customarily also holds the presidency of the UAE, the office is de facto hereditary. The president is also supreme commander of the UAE Armed Forces and chairman of the Supreme Council and Supreme Petroleum Council.

To note, the vice president/prime minister is the head of government of the United Arab Emirates. While not required by the UAE Constitution, historically the Ruler (other than in the case of Sheikh Maktoum bin Rashid from 1971–79, when he was Deputy Ruler) of Dubai has served as the prime minister.

70 Amina Al Rustamani, conversation with the author, January 13, 2015.

71 Pranay Gupte, *Dubai: The Making of a Megapolis* (New Delhi: Penguin Books India, 2011), 92–93.

72 Graeme Wilson, *Rashid's Legacy* (London: Media Prima, 2006), 219–200.

73 Mirza Al Sayegh, conversation with the author, February 6, 2015.

Chapter Nine

74 "Becoming a Leader," Sheikh Mohammed's official website, accessed August 1, 2015.

75 Boris Groysberg and Michael Slind, "Leadership Is a Conversation," *Harvard Business Review*, June 2012.

76 Rudolph Giuliani, *Leadership* (New York: Miramax, 2005).

Chapter Ten

77 Pranay Gupte, *Dubai: The Making of a Megapolis* (New Delhi: Penguin Books India, 2011), 168.

78 Graeme Wilson, *Rashid's Legacy* (London: Media Prima, 2006), 71.

79 Shane McGinley, "Emirates Sees 52 Percent Surge in Profit, Despite Unrest," *Arabian Business*, May 10, 2011.

80 Mohamed Alabbar, interview by Steve Harvey, *Emirates World Interviews*, January 2015.

81 Osman Sultan, conversation with the author, February 19, 2014.

82 The body that provides higher supervision and coordination between all government departments in Dubai, and follows up on their activities to make sure they are in line with the strategic development directions.

83 Lionel Barber, Roula Khalaf, and Simeon Kerr, interview with *Financial Times*, November 16, 2010.

Chapter Eleven

84 Emaar Press Release, "The Dubai Mall Is the 'Centre of World Retail' Welcoming Record Eighty Million Visitors in 2014," February 10, 2015.

85 P. M. Fitts and M. I. Posner, *Human Performance* (Belmont, CA: Brooks/Cole Publishing Company, 1967).

86 Mohamed Alabbar, interview by Steve Harvey, *Emirates World Interviews*, January 2015.

87 Raja Trad, conversation with the author, February 18, 2014.

88 Pranay Gupte, *Dubai: The Making of a Megapolis* (New Delhi: Penguin Books India, 2011), 182.

89 Mohammed bin Rashid Al Maktoum, M-Government Announcement, May 22, 2013.

90 Mohammed bin Rashid Al Maktoum, *My Vision* (Dubai: Motivate Publishing, 2012), 18.

91 Negar Azimi, "The Teaching Cure," *New York Times*, September 21, 2008.

92 "Innovate or Stagnate," His Highness Sheikh Mohammed bin

Rashid's LinkedIn page, last modified February 5, 2015, https://www.linkedin.com/pulse/innovate-stagnate-hh-sheikh-mohammed-bin-rashid-al-maktoum.

93 Mohammed bin Rashid Al Maktoum, question-and-answer session at the first "UAE Government Summit," February 11, 2013.

94 Mohammed bin Rashid Al Maktoum, speech for the "Sheikh Mohammed bin Rashid Al Maktoum Arab Administration Award and Dubai Government Excellence Programme," April 17, 2002.

Chapter Twelve

95 Graeme Wilson, *Rashid's Legacy* (London: Media Prima, 2006), 342.

96 Mirza Al Sayegh, conversation with the author, February 5, 2015.

97 Mohammed bin Rashid Al Maktoum, question-and-answer session at the first "UAE Government Summit," February 11, 2013.

98 Pranay Gupte, *Dubai: The Making of a Megapolis* (New Delhi: Penguin Books India, 2011), 190.

99 Staff writer, "Dubai Excellence Programme Has Potential," *Gulf News*, May 11, 2008.

100 Mohammed bin Rashid Al Maktoum, remarks at the World Economic Forum, Jordan, May 16, 2004.

101 "Women," UAE Interact website, accessed July 23, 2015, http://www.uaeinteract.com/society/women.asp.

Conclusion

102 Mohammed bin Rashid Al Maktoum, question-and-answer session at the first "UAE Government Summit," February 11, 2013.

103 Mohammed bin Rashid Al Maktoum, remarks at the World Economic Forum, Jordan, May 16, 2004.

BIBLIOGRAPHY

2012 International Council of Shopping Centres (ICSC) research report.

Ahmed Bahrozyan, conversation with the author, April 26, 2015.

Ahmed bin Butti, conversation with the author, December 19, 2012.

Ahmed Hassan Al Shaikh, "Is Dubai's Competitive Advantage Sustainable? A Study of Strategic Planning in Dubai 1996 to 2010." PhD diss., Coventry University, 2012.

Ahmed Hassan Al Shaikh, conversation with the author, April 25, 2013.

Alexander Cornwell, "Dubai World Central Airport Opens to Passengers," *Gulf News*, October 26, 2013.

Amina Al Rustamani, conversation with the author, January 13, 2015.

CBRE News, "Dubai Retains Second Position for International Retailer Representation for Fourth Consecutive Year," CBRE, the world's largest real estate investment manager, last modified May 18, 2015.

Dubai Plan 2021 website, accessed July 17, 2015.

Dubai Tourism Press Release, "Dubai Welcomes 12.2 International Visitors in 2014," May 3, 2015.

Emaar Press Release, "The Dubai Mall Is the 'Centre of World Retail' Welcoming Record Eighty Million Visitors in 2014," February 10, 2015.

Gary Chapman, conversation with the author, October 23, 2014.

Gerald Lawless, conversation with the author, March 25, 2014.

Graeme Wilson, *Rashid's Legacy* (London: Media Prima, 2006).

"Interview: Zayan Ghandour," Visit Dubai website, accessed August 1, 2015.

"Into the Twenty-First Century: A Strategic Plan to Build a Fully Diversified and Prosperous Economy," Government of Dubai, Department of Economic Development.

Linda Mahoney, conversation with the author, January 6, 2015.

Lionel Barber, Roula Khalaf, and Simeon Kerr, interview with *Financial Times*, November 16, 2010.

Malcolm Wall Morris, conversation with the author, April 30, 2013.

Maurice Flanagan, conversation with the author, July 2010.

Mirza Al Sayegh, conversation with the author, February 6, 2015.

Mohamed Alabbar, interview by Steve Harvey, *Emirates World Interviews*, January 2015.

Mohammed bin Rashid Al Maktoum, *40 Poems from the Desert* (Dubai: Motivate Publishing, 2011).

Mohammed bin Rashid Al Maktoum, *Flashes of Thought* (Dubai: Motivate Publishing, 2013).

Mohammed bin Rashid Al Maktoum, *My Vision* (Dubai: Motivate Publishing, 2012).

Mohammed bin Rashid Al Maktoum, remarks at the World Economic Forum, Jordan, May 16, 2004.

Mohammed bin Rashid Al Maktoum, Twitter page, modified May 23, 2015.

Mohammed bin Rashid Al Maktoum, question-and-answer session at the first "UAE Government Summit," February 11, 2013.

Nick Webster, "Women of the UAE: Mariana Garcia Garza," *The National*, May 17, 2015.

Osman Sultan, conversation with the author, February 19, 2014.

Paul Griffiths, conversation with the author, July 10, 2014.

P. M. Fitts and M. I. Posner, *Human Performance* (Brooks/Cole Publishing Company: Belmont, CA), 1967.

Pranay Gupte, *Dubai: The Making of a Megapolis* (New Delhi: Penguin Books India, 2011).

Raja Trad, conversation with the author, February 18, 2014.

Ram Charan, Stephen Drotter, and James Noel. *The Leadership Pipeline: How to Build the Leadership Powered Company* (San Francisco: Jossey-Bass, 2001).

Sami Al Mufleh, conversation with the author, December 29, 2014.

Shakir Husain, "The Pillars of Society: Farid Mohammad Ahmad," *Gulf News*, September 30, 2008.

Shane McGinley, "Emirates Sees 52 Percent Surge in Profit, Despite Unrest," *Arabian Business*, May 10, 2011.

Shane McGinley, "Interview: DIFC Courts Chief Mark Beer," *Arabian Business*, November 2, 2013.

Sheikh Mohammed bin Rashid Al Maktoum's official website, accessed August 1, 2015.

Stephen Bradley and Pankaj Ghemawat, "Wal*Mart Stores, Inc.," HBS No. 9-794-024 (Boston: Harvard Business School Publishing, 2002).

Steve Kroft, Interview with Mohammed bin Rashid Al Maktoum, *60 Minutes*, October 14, 2007.

"The Airport of the Future," Dubai Airport's 2050 Plan.

Tim Clark, speech for Bureau International des Expositions, October 22, 2013.

WAM Press Release, July 5, 2014.

WAM, "UAE Ranks First in World for Respecting Women," *Gulf News*, April 27, 2014.

Yuwa Hedrick-Wong and Desmond Choong, "2014 Global Destination Cities Index," *MasterCard Worldwide Insights*, 2014.

ABOUT THE AUTHOR

Dr. Tommy Weir is one of the foremost authorities on leadership in the Emerging Markets. As founder of the Dubai-based Emerging Markets Leadership Center (EMLC), Dr. Weir provides CEOs and other high-level leaders with trusted leadership advice.

Having helped more than 3,000 executives achieve peak performance, Dr. Tommy is equipped with an arsenal of rare insights that place him in high demand as a CEO coach, author, speaker, and advisor on senior executive leadership. Success stories include Fortune 500 companies, governments, and newly established corporations in Africa, Asia, and the Middle East.

A thinker, speaker, and writer to the core, Dr. Weir holds a doctorate in strategic leadership from Regent University. He is a leadership columnist and is the author of *10 Tips for Leading in the Middle East*, which was voted the #2 best book of 2014 by the *Wall Street Journal*'s readers poll. He is also the author of *Going Global*, *The CEO Shift*, and *The Cheeseburger Theory and Other Leadership Observations*.

For more information, visit www.tommyweir.com.